Ronald Williams was born in R‍
Rossall School in Lancashire, a‍   ‍ʌ
College Cambridge, he won a Tre‍   ‍ʋn the
Marquis of Montrose in 1960. Betw‍   ‍‥s a member
of the Diplomatic Service and served i‍   ‍ʋre, Budapest and
Nairobi. His first book, *Montrose: Caval‍   ‍ning*, was published in
1975. From 1980 to 1997 he worked in th‍   ‍ʋrestry sector and from 1987
to 1997 was Executive Director of the Forestry Industry Council of Great
Britain. In 1998 he became Chief Executive of the Publishers Association.

He was appointed OBE in 1991 and is a Fellow of the Royal Society for
the Encouragement of Arts, Manufactures and Commerce (FRSA). In
addition to Scottish history, he has a passion for fly-fishing and his interests include archaeology, photography, walking, travel and Real Tennis.
When not in Scotland, Ronald Williams lives in a small Hampshire village
in the valley of the River Test.

Sons of the Wolf is the sequel to *The Lords of the Isles* and *The Heather
and The Gale*, which are also published by House of Lochar.

Sons of the Wolf

SONS OF THE WOLF

*Campbells and MacGregors
and the Cleansing of the
Inland Glens*

Ronald Williams

British Cataloguing in Publication Data
A catalogue record for this book is available from the British Library

ISBN 1 899863 42 7

First published by House of Lochar 1998

Typeset in Ehrhardt by XL Publishing Services, Tiverton
Printed in Great Britain by SRP Ltd, Exeter
for House of Lochar, Isle of Colonsay, Argyll PA61 7YR, Scotland

Contents

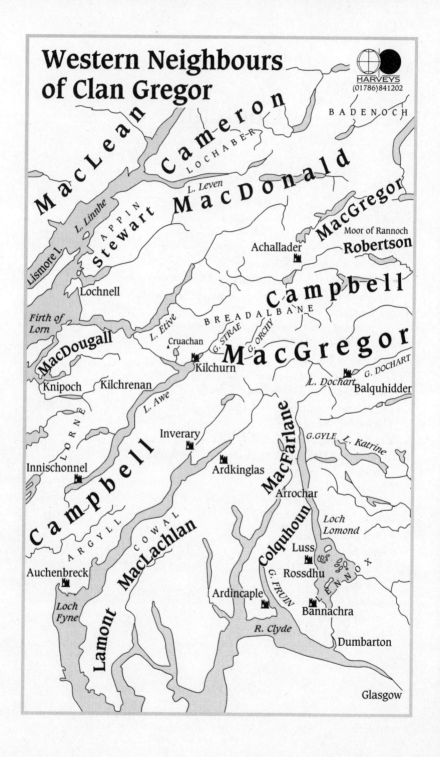

Eastern Neighbours of Clan Gregor

CHAPTER I

Campbells and MacGregors

Lorne of the mountains and lonely sea-arms,
Triple-peaked Cruachan, Starav and Ime,
Land of MacCailein, MacDougall, MacGregor
Still there is keening in empty Glenstrae.

Kilchurn Castle stands on a green promontory at the northern end of Loch
Awe, sentinel over the land where the three glens meet, and watched over
by the peaks of Ben Cruachan. The building is ruinous and unpeopled
now, the floors grass-grown and its halls open to the wind and sky, but its
size and position attest to the power and ambition of the Campbell lords
who built it, and who ruled and oppressed the people of the inland glens
over which they claimed superiority.

Awe of Cruachan – *Cruachan Beann, mo Cruachan Beann* – was once a
part of the Campbells' unity, the core of their homeland, their watchword
and rallying cry. But although the elemental landscape may still inspire or
exhilarate, it can convey no understanding of righteous or unjust causes.
The moods change with sun and rain, mist and shadow. The colours alter-
nate according to the seasons. Although the scene is wild, the imprint of
man is everywhere around – in the loss of the ancient deer forest, the
poverty of vegetation after centuries of sheep, and the relics of abandoned
settlement cleared by epidemic or eviction. It is in the old clan burial
grounds and the art of the carved stones; it is in older monastic ruins and
older still, in the iron-age hill forts, ancient duns, and cairns that tell of
dead warriors who fought and fell in long forgotten forays during the early
history of Lorne.

But these too are silent witness. There is more to be learned in the harp-
song and the music, in the fierce pibrochs of the ancient clans and in their
airs of lamentation. Most of all there is the call of memory which in a
culture based upon the remembered word was of particular importance to
the early Gaels and who, listening to the old stories recited by their bards,
would boast of their ancient glories, recall past feuds or treacheries and
brood upon unforgiven wrongs.

These stories do not sit quietly by the picturesque ruins of Kilchurn or the tranquility of the water that laps against the loch shore. Terrible things were done or planned here – amounting to a ruthless ethnic cleansing of the glens and the intended extermination of an entire clan.

*   *   *

Towards the southern end of Loch Awe, on a small island close by the shore, the castle of Innischonnel was the original cradle of Campbell power in Lorne. The earliest lords of Innischonnel were the O'Duins, a family of Irish origin descended from a certain Diarmid O'Duin, himself a nephew of Fionn MacCaul, son of the High King of Ireland. In the 13th century the heiress of Duncan O'Duin of Innischonnel married a knight of Strathclyde or possibly Norman descent called Sir Colin Cambeul. From him the later Campbell chiefs inherited their appellation of MacCailein Mor – "Great Son of Colin" – while the clan also called themselves the "Children of Diarmid" as recalling their kinship to that illustrious Irish ancestor.

A red granite slab at Kilchrenan records the death of Sir Colin, killed by a MacDougall arrow during a skirmish at the String of Lorne in 1294. His son, Sir Neil Campbell, was a contemporary and companion of Sir William Wallace, and during the later war of independence switched allegiance from Balliol to Bruce and profited from the redistribution of lands forfeited by the MacDougalls, Lamonts and others of the Comyn faction. Thus the gratitude of Bruce laid the foundation of the Campbells' empire in the western highlands.

To Sir Neil's son, the second Sir Colin, the King granted "one free barony of Lochow" which included most of Argyll between Lorne and Loch Fyne. In Cowal, the Campbells obtained the baronies of Ardkinglas, Ardgarten, and Kilmun on Holy Loch. Acquisitive by nature and expansionist by policy, during the 14th and 15th centuries they steadily amassed a great tract of territory stretching from Cawdor in Moray through Breadalbane and Argyll and as far south as Ayr.[1]

As their wealth and power increased, marriage into the great Scottish families brought the opportunity of lowland honours. The second Sir Colin had married a sister of The Bruce. His great grandson, Duncan Campbell of Lochow married a daughter of the Regent Albany who was governing Scotland during the captivity of James I, and was made Lord Campbell in 1445. For services to James I after his return he was rewarded with a grant of the peninsula of Roseneath from Albany's forfeited estates, and his grandson, another Sir Colin, was created Earl of Argyll in 1457.

In Gaelic this was translated as *Iarla Oirthir Gaedhel* – "Earl of the Sea-coasts of the Gael". Within the clan he remained the MacCailein Mor, and these several titles reflected the critical combination of feudal lord and highland chiefship upon which the Campbells' power was methodically constructed.

Seven years later the Earl of Argyll obtained the ancient district of Lorne itself after plotting the assassination of the Stewart incumbent and marrying the heiress. The Stewarts of Lorne also owned Glenlyon and the marriage of a second daughter to Argyll's uncle (Campbell of Glenorchy) secured that territory within the Campbells' expanding control. In 1464 Argyll was made hereditary Master of the Royal Household, and in 1473 he was appointed Justiciar of Scotland, Chamberlain, and Sheriff and Baillie of Argyll under Royal Charter. James III also gave him a Commission of Lieutenancy with vice-regal powers throughout Argyll. In 1474 he was granted Inveraray in Lochow on the shore of Loch Fyne which succeeded Innischonnel as the centre of the Campbell power, from where they could control their highland territory while yet maintaining their political communications with the lowlands.

Argyll repaid these favours by siding with the band of Scottish nobles who hounded James III to death and placed James IV upon the throne (gratitude was rarely a Campbell trait). His reward was an extension of his vice-regal powers in the highlands and increasing influence at the Scottish court. His son, Archibald, 2nd Earl of Argyll, was appointed Justice General of the kingdom, and from this time, in regions where MacCailein Mor had sway, the lowland law would run with Campbell order.

"Conques and keep things conquest"[2] wrote their chronicler. What the Campbells took they kept, and how they took it was without scruple. When the last Lamont Thane of Cawdor died in 1495, leaving only a baby girl, the Earl of Argyll obtained her wardship from James IV and tried to force the infant's betrothal to his own son. When the family resisted, the Campbells raided Kilravock in strength and abducted the child. Tradition has it that the girl's mother branded her with a red-hot key and the nurse bit off one of the baby's finger joints to prove her identity thereafter, but the Campbells boasted that so long as there was a red haired lass in Lorne they would not lack an heiress to Cawdor. The girl was later married to Argyll's third son John, from whom the Campbells of Cawdor trace their descent.

Meanwhile, marching with Lorne to the east was the district of Glenorchy and the region known as Breadalbane – a tract of land extending from Glendochart and Glenlyon through Lawers and the old estates of

3

Balloch (Kenmore) at the end of Loch Tay, and northwards into the wild bounds of Rannoch. In 1432, Duncan Campbell of Lochow had granted lands in Glenorchy to his younger son, Sir Colin, a crusader and Knight of St John, who built Kilchurn Castle to guard the Pass of Brander and keep the north-east gateways to the Campbells' country. He later acquired the lands of Lawers and Glendochart – shared with the Campbells of Strachur and other cadets of Lochow – and his son would obtain Balloch and Glenlyon together with hereditary rights in the districts around Loch Tay. Established in their stronghold of Kilchurn, the Campbells of Glenorchy were poised to pursue their eastward ambition among the inland glens.

* * *

The MacGregors – the Gregarach – were the foremost tribe among the *Siol Alpin* – the group of clans (which also included the Grants, MacKinnons, MacQuarries, MacNabs and MacAulays) who claimed descent from Kenneth MacAlpine, the Dalriadic King who in 843 assumed the crown of all Scotland and established himself in the ancient Pictish capital at Scone. Thus their motto *"S'rioghal mo dhream"* – "Royal is my blood". Their badge was the pine tree.

Before the Scottish Wars of Independence, the clan appear to have been in possession of a large part of Perthshire, and there was a time when Glenorchy, Glenlyon and Glenstrae were known as "MacGregor's Glens". Their 13th-century progenitor may have been one Ey Urchaych – Hugh of Glenorchy – who was possibly granted those lands by the Earl of Ross after he had received them from Alexander III (died 1249), but by the late 15th century branches of the family had also established themselves in Glenstrae, Roro, Balloch, Balquhidder, Ardcoille, and Glengyle. The clan thus became scattered across a vast and ill-defined tract of the central highlands, encompassing Breadalbane and west through the MacNabs' territory in Glendochart and the homelands of Glenlochy, Glenorchy and Glenstrae to march with the Campbells' country of Lochow; north through Glenlyon to the wilderness of Rannoch; eastwards around Tummel into the lands of the Murrays of Atholl; along Tay and Strathearn, and south to the Trossachs and via Glenfalloch to Loch Lomondside and the gateway to the lowlands.

This territory supported a population of several thousand people among whom the Gregarach were probably a majority. Most were gathered in small settlements of turf built houses (only the chiefs would have had stone built dwellings) dependent upon the products of the land about.

The sheltering mountains enclosed common hill pastures for quite substantial herds of cattle, sheep and goats, while the lower soils were allocated to growing oats and barley. Left unmolested, it was basically a subsistence culture. Most critically, it was socially and economically land dependent.

There were no maps of this country. The intricate geography of the glens and passes was known only to the native population. Travel was by foot or pony-back, carriage by pack-mules along paths, deer runs, or the few drove roads – cattle-trod tracks over heather, bog and bridgeless rivers, better known to reivers than more lawful traffic. Travellers were usually seasonal and few. MacGregor packmen might visit lowland towns such as Dumbarton to trade or buy necessary lowland goods – salt, iron nails, knives and such – but the lowlanders had no material or aesthetic incentive to venture into the dangerous country among the forbidding hills. Such traffic as took place was largely conducted by those whose business obliged them – the factors of the bordering estates collecting rent or other dues, or foresters upon the Royal business; or by such as tinkers, toolmakers, pedlars, who sold basic necessities (and the occasional luxury), and the gaberlunzie men who carried the news and made a living from these remote communities. And even they probably penetrated only into the more accessible glens.

Highlands and lowlands were physically, politically and culturally distinct. To the lowlander, the highlands presented a mountainous backdrop to an ordered world – a wild fastness of unknown geography or extent, for all purposes a foreign land where English was not spoken, and which was peopled by wild and lawless clansmen who were given to brigandage and could sweep down on a wild night to raid and plunder and then disappear again into their remote glens among the mists and impenetrable mountains.

The language of lowland government documents reflected a contempt for highlanders who were regarded as uncivilised, barbaric, sub-human even, and these extreme opinions were justification to deprive the clansmen of their ancestral rights, to order policies of eviction and even the extermination of entire populations. Such views were often encouraged by those like the Earl of Argyll, who, being also the MacCailein Mor, had interests in both these worlds and saw advantage in promoting disturbance among the highland clans as a means of acquiring further jurisdiction. Stories of highland disorder – false or genuine, instigated or spontaneous – were ever in the government's ears and lowland sentiment towards the clans grew progressively more antagonistic.

Certainly, during the 15th and 16th centuries there was endemic disorder in the highlands. Geographical conditions made it virtually impossible to enforce the law and the central government exercised little authority. Language differences meant that lowland influence hardly penetrated into the highland glens.

With the forfeiture of the Lordship of the Isles and the break-up of the old Celtic earldoms, many clans previously subordinate and therefore under some kind of order, began to pursue independent policies of aggrandisement or preservation – leading inevitably to the unchecked pursuit of latent rivalries and feuds amongst themselves. This dispersal of authority, coming at a time when the old clan system itself was being surreptitiously undermined by feudal laws of tenure, made them vulnerable to the predations of the Campbells and other "charter lords" who astutely capitalised on the weakness of the central government to acquire for themselves the powers of law enforcement which they bent to serve their own dynastic and territorial ends.

In the early 12th century during the reigns of Alexander I and David I, large numbers of Normans had settled in Scotland by invitation. They brought with them the notions and customs of Norman feudalism, the rights of primogeniture, and the holding of land in feu and upon written charter.

This feudalism co-existed with the older Gaelic clan system. The two interacted in a variety of ways, and in some lowland situations came to merge. The old native Celtic Earls had held the hereditary allegiance of populations within their territories and had been able to impose order and provide protection. When later, the Crown failed to provide such protection, war and anarchy broke society into smaller groups who, for reasons of kinship or feudal dependence, adhered to a local chief and organised themselves into clans of a "quasi feudal" type. Among some Gaelic communities feudalism became grafted onto the former clan system – sometimes by imposition.

This was possible because there were certain similarities between the two systems. Both were established on theories of landholding, and both gave to individual dependants lands to occupy and protection in their occupation either through kinship with the clan chief or by contract with the feudal lord. There were, however, certain significant differences which affected a clan as a whole. Within the feudal system, if the Crown granted a baron's lands to a new holder, it also automatically transferred the allegiance of all the tenants. Under the clan system, allegiance could only be transferred with the clansman's individual consent – which he did by giving his bond of "manrent" (service) and his *"calp"*(on his death the payment of the best beast in his byre to his acknowledged chief). It was therefore desirable that the clan chief should also be the feudal superior of the lands occupied by his clansmen, but significantly, this was not always the case.

The potential conflict of loyalties between kinship and feudal title could be complicated by the custom that while the clan chief in all clans represented their common ancestry, the office was hereditary to the family and not the individual. The system was aristocratic in that the successor or *Tanist* was elected from among the chief's close relatives, but it excluded feudal primo-geniture as an automatic principle of succession.

The most important differences lay in the notion of land-holding itself. While the feudal system treated land as personal property, it was Gaelic rule and custom that clan land belonged to the clan as a whole and not to a person. The chief had superiority of it, but only in the name of the clan as its "father". The land was held in trust, divided among the chief's near relatives who in turn sub-divided the arable land by lot among the clansmen (pasture was held in common). The clansmen raised crops, cattle and fighting men. Leases were verbal and rents paid in kind.

Claims to the clan land itself could be various. In oldest times the Gaels reckoned to hold their land under allodial title (from God and not under the law) – which in effect meant by prior settlement and sword right – *Coir a cleadhaimh* – or by verbal grant in front of witnesses during the period of the Lordship of the Isles. Formal written charters to land did not exist during the earlier Celtic period, but after the spread of Norman feudalism and particularly from the reign of Robert the Bruce, the principal chiefs were put under pressure to accept charters in their own name for their clan's land. Large numbers succumbed to charter acceptance rather than lose their clan's land to an alien overlord. Some, however, were irreconcilable and continued to occupy their lands by strength without the legal security of holding a charter to it.

Those more "backward" clans who neglected to obtain this safeguard became increasingly vulnerable to the predations of the feudal "charter lords" who used the intricacies of lowland law which the naive highlanders did not properly understand – charters, mortgages, the buying up of debts, new tenancies, the exploitation of dormant claims – to further their own territorial expansion among their neighbours' lands.

The consequence of this encroachment was not always eviction in the

7

first instance and in many cases the clansmen were allowed to go on living on their ancestral lands as "kindly tenants" without any formal legal title. Sometimes the clansmen successfully resisted attempts to dispossess them and maintained their traditional rights by a "strong hand".

However, where the clansmen were dispossessed and evicted from the clan's land by a feudal "charter lord" they had no recourse but to live by brigandage and plunder as their only means of livelihood, and not surprisingly they often retaliated by attacking and robbing the new owners of the farms which had been taken from them. The resulting disorder was represented to the lowland government as further evidence of the ferocity and intractability of the primitive highland people, and distracted Kings were persuaded to put yet more powerful legal instruments into the hands of the "charter lords" who offered to take upon themselves the responsibility for pacifying the highland regions.

In some cases these lords were responsible for the disorder in the first place, since the "broken men" who had lost their land were a ready army for them to use in the pursuit of their own feuds without danger or the risk of blame to themselves. Outlaw bands could be induced to commit "hership and strouthrief" – murder and fire-raising – with promises of help and shelter afterwards, but if anything went wrong, the great men could repudiate or desert them when it suited. Alternatively, clans could be incited to raid or retaliate against a neighbour, giving the "charter lord" an opportunity to step in to keep the peace armed with Letters of Fire and Sword and a charter to the victims' land. In manipulating the highlanders in this way, cynical predators like the Campbells were able to exploit the naive trust which the Gaels traditionally placed in a great man's word.

At the same time they were in fact encouraging the clansmen to engage in activities that were historically congenial to them. Highland landlords themselves had never been greatly concerned to put down disorder. Every man was ready to defend his own property, but few would interfere with another man's right to lift cattle from another clan's district, and the lowlands were considered a land where any highland man might take his prey. The "Herd Widdifous" – the "Gallows Herd" – returning from a raid were traditionally allowed to pass through areas unchallenged (so long as they paid the landlord a percentage of the stolen cattle). Cattle raiding was held to be quite distinct from ordinary theft. Since Celtic times it had been looked on as a sport or test of prowess while a little bloodletting won prestige and demonstrated the vigour of the clan. The time for raiding was around the end of September during the Michaelmas moon when the cattle were in prime condition. The MacFarlanes of Arrochar, who claimed descent from the 12th century Celtic earls of Lennox, were such notorious raiders that the Michaelmas moon was known as MacFarlane's Lantern and they boasted of their reputation in their pipe tune *Thogail nam Bo* (Lifting the cattle):

> *We drive the cattle through the glens*
> *Through the corries, woods and bens*
> *Through the sleet or misty rain.*
> *When the moon is shining low*
> *By frozen loch and drifted snow*
> *Stealthily and bold we go*
> *Though small our hope of gain.*

Besides the regular occupation of cattle raiding, feuding was endemic – Atholl and Argyll, Argyll and Colquhoun, Menzies and Stewart of Garth, Stewarts and MacIvors, Drummonds and Murrays, and others such as MacDonalds and Camerons from Lochaber ready to plunder indiscriminately.

It was a fatal mistake of the highlanders that clans like the Gregarach did not understand the cynical morality of the "charter lords" and the new significance of the written word and legal loop-hole. When they did it was too late, because it became a strategic objective of Campbell expansion to prevent them from obtaining legal feudal title to any of their land.

In 1597, provoked by violent feuding between MacDonalds and MacLeans in the west and further disorder in Strathnaver, the government of James VI would decree that all chiefs and lairds should produce titles to the lands they occupied, and stand surety for the behaviour of their clansmen or feudal dependants. In the same year, the Privy Council ruled that no part of the highlands should be thenceforth "disponit in feu, tak, or otherwise but to lowland men". Men without titles fought the more fiercely for what they held. The Gallows Herd recklessly continued their cattle raiding. Government Writs of Fire and Sword authorised ferocious reprisals – "slaughter, mutilation, fire raising and other inconveniencies". By these commissions against their highland neighbours, the Earls of Argyll, Huntly, Seaforth, Sutherland, Lennox and others were able to cloak their own predations behind the substance of royal authority.

All these things would contribute to the MacGregors' downfall. In such circumstances, to be lordless was to have no protection, no powerful voice in the Council, no recognition under the law, and no shelter from pursuit.

To be landless allowed only the two alternatives – to hold by sword-right or run with the "broken men". To be such and friendless also was to invite extinction. Lordless, landless and with no hope of betterment, the Gregarach would display a particular defiance.

CHAPTER 2

The Early History of the Clan Gregor (1296–1570)

Glenorchy's proud mansion, Kilchurn with her towers,
Glenstrae and Glenlyon no longer are ours –
We're landless, landless, landless, Gregarach,
Landless, landless, landless.

The MacGregors were not the first or the only tribe to inhabit the region of the three glens. An old highland saying claims that it was the Fletchers who first raised smoke and boiled water in Glenorchy – a way perhaps of describing them as an aboriginal or pre-Celtic people who came to be called after their craft rather than assuming any formal clan designation. The name in Gaelic – *Mac an Fhleistear* – means "Son of the Arrowmaker", and in possible confirmation of this traditional occupation the area retains evidence of arrow making over a thousand years before the founding of Albain Dalriada.[3]

The bow was favoured for hunting as for war, and an old rhyme describes the highland archer's equipment and its origin:

> *Bow from yew of Esragin*
> *Eagle feather from Loch Treig,*
> *Yellow wax from Galway town,*
> *And arrow-head made by MacPhederan.*

Similarly, the small neighbouring valley of Glenoe which skirts the flank of Cruachan north from Kilchurn Castle was from earliest times the home of the MacIntyres, called "The Sons of the Carpenter" – who were also traditionally foresters to the Lords of Lorne, and better known as hereditary pipers to the MacDonald of Clanranald and later to the Menzies chief.

Glenoe was poor and thus uncoveted, so that the MacIntyres seem to have been left in relative peace, accepting their dependence upon the powerful neighbours whom they served.

Glenlyon, which would feature prominently in the MacGregors' story, was also populated from an early date. Extending some thirty five miles in all, it is the longest of the highland glens, overshadowed for most of its length by the great peaks of Schiehallion (sacred mountain of the ancient Picts) to the north, and Ben Lawers to the south. Ancient occupation is evidenced by the circular iron-age forts that guard the passes north into Rannoch and south toward the Tay which tradition associates with the legendary dark-age hero Fionn and his nine thousand warriors who manned these defences.

> *Twelve castles had Fionn*
> *In the crooked glen of the stones.*

The names of two of them are still remembered – *Casteal coin a Bhacain* – "The Castle of the Dogs' Stake" – where the Fians are said to have fed their hunting pack, and nearby, *Caisteal an Duibh* – "The Castle of the Dark Hero". Their association with Fionn in the tales of highland sean-nachies make them perhaps the oldest forts in Britain about which a living tradition is still preserved. (Fionn is believed to have lived during the latter part of the third century, and the standing stone in the field behind the school at Killin is said to mark the place where he lies buried.)

Mid-way up Glenlyon, the *Craig Fhiannaidh* – a huge boulder – marks the place where St Eonan (St Adomnan, St Columba's hagiographer) is said to have turned back the plague in 664AD. It became the judgement mound, where local chieftains met to seal oral agreements according to Gaelic custom. In about 1488 it was the scene of a fierce battle between the Stewarts of Garth and MacIvors from Rannoch for control of the glen, in which the Stewarts were victorious. Nearby place names still recall the fight and the final killing ground where the MacIvors died: *Lech na Cuaran* – where each Stewart clansman left a shoe so that afterwards the survivors could count the number missing: *Ruskith* where they unsheathed their swords, and *Laggan a chatha* where the fight took place. Eight miles further up the glen is *Camus na Carn* – 'The Field of Cairns' – where the MacIvors made their last stand and 150 of them are said to be buried here. The old clan seannachies told that the river ran red with blood so that the name Glenlyon – "The Glen of the Tinged River" – dates from that day. In fact the name was much older.

There are traces too of another battle between a warrior called Black John of the Spears who is described in Gaelic poetry as "Chief of Glenlyon", "a King at lifting cattle" and "the white-toothed falcon of the three glens", and a band of marauding Chisolms from Strathglass. Six of

Black John's seven sons were killed beside him but the Chisolm chief was eventually slain by a marksman's arrow at the place still called *Clach an T'Siolach* – "Chisolm's Stone" – on the hill of Kerrowmore.

This Black John of the Spears may have been an early MacGregor, since he built the church of Brenudh (St Brandon) which became a traditional burial place of the MacGregors of Roro.

Finally there was Glenstrae, of these valleys the most empty, running northwards from the head of Loch Awe – a place of green shadows along Strae Water under the looming slopes of Cruachan and Ben Eunaich. The main area of settlement was at the foot of the glen around Stronmelochan (Stronmilchan) in the Strath of Orchy, and the community gathered at the old hamlet of Dysart (Dalmally) where the MacGregors of Glenstrae were buried in the old church under a cyst of stones on the north side of the high altar. However, today nothing remains to recall their occupation.

*   *   *

In 1296, the year in which Balliol was deposed and Edward I claimed the crown of Scotland for himself, John, son of Malcolm of Glenorchy was captured fighting against the English, and died leaving only a daughter called Mariota to inherit.

Mariota was married by John Campbell, a younger son of the MacCailein Mor (who was then living at Innischonnel) and when this marriage produced no surviving child to adopt the maternal inheritance as chief of the clan, the Campbells claimed the superiority of Glenorchy for themselves.

Faced with the prospect of feudal vassalage to a Campbell lord with whom they had no blood relationship or leavening of kinship, the clansmen of Glenorchy elected a grandson of Malcolm called Gregor of the Golden Bridles to be their chief, and he became the name-father of the MacGregors.

Gregor repudiated the Campbells' pretensions and under his leadership the clan continued to occupy by sword-right the land they claimed by immemorial possession. The record of John of Glenorchy in siding with Sir William Wallace against the English might have counted in the clan's favour, but during the subsequent wars of independence the MacGregors probably fought for John of Lorne against Robert the Bruce, and so unlike their Campbell neighbours they got no profit from that King's gratitude. (The MacGregors demonstrated an unfortunate talent for picking a losing side.)

Gregor was succeeded by his son, John the One-eyed who lived until 1390. John the One-eyed had three sons: Patrick who succeeded him, John Dow from whom the MacGregors of Glenstrae, and Gregor from whom the MacGregors of Roro.

Although this was a turbulent period in Scottish history during the captivity in England of James I, for much of the 15th century, despite the claim to Glenorchy the MacGregors and the Campbells appear to have co-existed and the Gregarach sustained relatively little harm. The MacGregor anthology of Gaelic poetry compiled by Sir James MacGregor, Dean of Lismore during the 16th century is even-handed in its treatment of the Campbells. One Campbell chief is complimented on his literary taste. Archibald, 2nd Earl of Argyll who was Chancellor of Scotland and was killed leading a highland contingent at the Battle of Flodden in 1513, is addressed "Thou Archibald who would refuse no man, thou art the Lugh (an ancient Celtic hero) of this latter time: thou Earl of Argyll be a champion triumphant!" Praise, understandably, is heaped upon MacGregor chieftains such as Black John of the Spears, but it is criticism of MacDonald of Clanranald which perhaps most reflects the disorder of the time: "It was you who stirred up evil in the Isles; thou didst impoverish her tribute and her sanctuary; thy behaviour has ever been a coward's".

Nevertheless, the seeds of future trouble were being planted as the Campbells' power increased and further expansion was the inevitable temptation. In 1432, Colin Campbell, the second son of the MacCailein Mor, was granted a charter to Glenorchy. He built Kilchurn Castle and his people began gradually to colonise the MacGregors' glens. In 1457 the MacCailein Mor was created 1st Earl of Argyll, and in 1464 he acquired the lands of Lorne after encompassing the murder of the incumbent. In 1499 the 2nd Earl of Argyll gained Cawdor by kidnapping the heiress. In 1492 Duncan Campbell of Glenorchy (the second Campbell laird) obtained the office of Baillie of the crown lands of Glenlyon and Glendochart, and by 1502 he had secured a charter to Glenlyon for himself. Empowered by Act of Parliament, together with Ewen Campbell of Strachur and other charter lords "for staunching of thiftrief and other enormities throw all the realm", he now had legal commission to pursue his ambitions among the MacGregors' lands over a wide area. In 1528 the office of Lord Justice General was made hereditary to the Earls of Argyll and from then on the Campbells controlled the courts.

"Hame's hamely, quo the deil when he found himself in the Court of Session".

While the Campbells grew, the Gregarach weakened. They possessed no legal charter to the lands which they occupied in Glenorchy and so were reduced to the status of tenants at will. Patrick, son of John the One-eyed, was forced to sell the lands of Auchinrevach in Strathfillan to Campbell of Glenorchy who thereby obtained a toehold in Breadalbane. Only in Glenstrae was the MacGregor chief a legal tenant of the Earl of Argyll – a situation which, if it enabled him to escape the predations of Campbell of Glenorchy, nevertheless put him at the disposal of the more powerful MacCailein Mor. However, as long as the clan remained united under the chief, the MacGregors were able to defend their lands with a strong hand. It became Campbell policy to seek to divide the clan.

Early in the 16th century, a younger son of MacGregor of Glenorchy called Dughall Cia Mor (Big Brown Dugall) ravished and then married a daughter of Colin Campbell of Glenorchy. Such rude courtship was not so uncommon in that time and highland reivers would regularly lift some women along with the beasts.(Sir Walter Scott would recall a highland woman telling him that her mother "had never seen her father till the night he brought her back from the Lennox with ten head of cattle and there had not been a happier couple in the country.")

The Campbells were politically reconciled to the match. Dughall Cia Mor was known for his energy and ambition. They encouraged his aspirations and although admitting that the claim was "not righteous", declared him to be the new chief of the Gregarach in the fair certainty that this would split the clan. They then set about the extermination of the true heirs.

The MacGregors of Glenorchy rose in arms – first against the impostor and then against Campbell evictions. The dispossessed Gregarach came to be called *Clann a Cheathaich* – Children of the Mist (or sometimes Sons of the Wolf). They took land if it was empty or shelter where they could and made a living by plundering the farms which had been taken from them. They spread through Breadalbane, Glendochart and into the Trossachs country, while the wilder spirits went north into the country around Rannoch – a vast wilderness of peat moss and remote ridges of rock and heather. Although parts of this region were technically within the jurisdiction of Menzies of Weem, Rannoch was an inaccessible and debatable land, never possessed by one clan but rather the haunt of caterans and broken men from every quarter. To the north was the territory of the Lochaber raiders where the dark woods of Badenoch and the ancient Caledonian Forest offered an inviolable refuge for outlaws – *Fear so cheann fo'n choille* – "The men whose head is under the wood". The disinherited

MacGregors lived mainly around the western shore of Loch Rannoch and on both banks of the River Gaur. They acquired some land at Stronfernan legally from the Clan Donnachaidh (Robertsons) and at Dunan as tenants of Menzies of that Ilk, but most they held by sword right of possession. They fortified a small island in Loch Rannoch and made it their stronghold.

Raiding out of Rannoch, the Children of the Mist now earned a reputation for brigandage so that they were denounced to the Privy Council as reivers, thieves, fire-raisers, murderers, and for all manner of crimes. Their history emerges through a list of Acts of the Privy Council by which commissions were granted to pursue the clan with fire and sword together with notices of various atrocities which in retaliation or despair, the Gregarach were reported to have committed.

Despite being widely scattered, the clan continued to display a remarkable unity and resilience so that many of the commissions were not implemented. In 1523 when the MacGregors of Dunan were causing particular nuisance, Sir Robert Menzies of Weem refused to obey the order of the Privy Council to bring them under control on the grounds that "MacGregor on force enterit the said Robertis landis of Rannoch and withaldis the samyn from him maisterfullie, and will nocht be put out be him of the saidis landis".[4] The Gregarach remained in Rannoch until in 1531 the King ordered the Earl of Atholl to drive them out. Atholl took the castle in the loch but vacated it after several months when the government refused to meet the cost of a garrison. The Gregarach regained possession.

Yet all the MacGregors were not inveterately at feud with their neighbours (perhaps because they raided beyond them) and in accordance with the highland culture based on a man's spoken bond, personalities had and would have a significant influence. Hence in 1537 Sir John Campbell, 4th of Glenorchy took Duncan MacGregor the Roro chieftain with his son and Gregor Dougalson of Balloch and his two brothers in his "tail" when he travelled to Paris for the wedding of James V to Madeleine de Valois – suggesting perhaps that there was no great enmity between that particular Campbell of Glenorchy and his MacGregor neighbours.

With the dispersal of the Glenorchy MacGregors, the chiefship appears to have passed to the Glenstrae branch, but the heir, Alasdair MacGregor had been brought up a ward of the Earl of Argyll and had been married to a daughter of Campbell of Ardkinglas – thus ensuring as they thought, a measure of Campbell control. During his minority, effective leadership of the clan was seized by a notorious marauder called Duncan Ladasach (the

Lordly) from Ardcoille, who established himself at the stronghold in Loch Rannoch and gathered a strong band of outlaws to raid into Glenorchy. "I lovit never justice nor yet law" Duncan Ladasach was said to have boasted. A poem, *Duncan Ladasach's Testament* (published within the Campbells' own account in *The Black Book of Taymouth* and therefore probably composed by one of his enemies) gives a contemporary if partisan view of some of his exploits.

> *In the nicht the loud coronach, God wit,*
> *Was at our tail with mony roustie akes:*
> *We had the kye, and they gat bot the glaiks.*

Under Duncan Ladasach the Gregarach acquired an evil reputation which would ever after be held against the clan to fuel lowland prejudice and make the Privy Council determine on their utter ruin. Inevitably the young chief of Glenstrae came under his influence also – frustrated perhaps by the constraints of Campbell tutelage or persuaded by the need to accomplish some exploit that would win back the loyalty of the scattered clansmen. Together they mounted an attack against Glenorchy:

> *I gart MacGregor wickedly pretend*
> *The house of Glenorchy to bring to ruin,*
> *Upon ane nicht to Glenlyon as they did wend,*
> *Baith young and auld that of that house was hend,*
> *With sudden fire we thought for to pursue,*
> *But they were wise, and weel our treason knew.*

Glenstrae next raided Strathbraan, burned the House of Trochry and kidnapped Struan Robertson, Chief of Clan Donnaidh. However, just when it seemed that the young MacGregor was settling into a career of "hership and rief", he suddenly died. His eldest son had been killed in one of these skirmishes, and his heir, Gregor Roy, was still a minor. In this situation, the Gregarach decided to confirm Duncan Ladasach as "Captain" of the clan and to appoint him Tutor to Gregor Roy (a reflection of the esteem in which the old brigand was held).

> *Their wit was weak, or else they wanted sleep,*
> *They gave the wolf the wether for to keep*

However, at about the same time, Sir Colin Campbell, called "The

Grey" succeeded to the lordship of Glenorchy, and taking advantage of the fact that the Glenstrae chief was still a child, began aggressively to impose his influence among the lesser clansmen who would normally have looked to The MacGregor for protection. By threats and promises Grey Colin induced a number of Glenstrae's people to sign bonds of "manrent" with him, by which they renounced their own chief and transferred their *calp* to Campbell of Glenorchy, swearing either to fight for him or at the least remain neutral if he should come to feud against Glenstrae.[5]

As Captain of the Gregarach during Gregor Roy's minority, Duncan Ladasach decided to discipline these renegade clansmen whose transfer of allegiance he viewed as treachery. One of these was a man called Alasdair Our who had "sold his highland birthright" for a lease of the lands of Morenish. On a November evening, Duncan and his eldest son Gregor rode to the house of Alasdair Our "at six hours at even under silence of night", dragged him outside and murdered him. They also took his purse for good measure. They then rode on to Killin where, according to the charges brought by Grey Colin, they murdered a piper called John MacBain against whom they bore some grudge.

Grey Colin for his own reputation's sake was bent on retribution and engaged various of his henchmen to capture or kill Duncan Ladasach and his sons, but their expeditions against the outlaw failed. Tradition has it that Grey Colin then resorted to treachery by pretending to a formal reconciliation. On 2nd May 1552 he signed a bond between himself and Duncan Ladasach together with his son Gregor declaring that he had forgiven them their crimes "the zeal of love and guid conscience moving me to the samyn", while they in turn granted him an escheat on all their goods on their death. It seems impossible to credit that either of the parties could have trusted the other, but according to one version of what happened next, Grey Colin invited Gregor to his castle at Finlarig and set an ambush for him on the way. Gregor broke through the Campbells and tried to escape by swimming the Lochay, but he was wounded and weak from loss of blood, so that his pursuers overtook and captured him. His horse was sent as a token for him with a message to Duncan Ladasach who was thus lured to Finlarig and imprisoned also. Whatever the truth of the tale, its end was certain. Duncan Ladasach and Gregor were beheaded at Balloch (Kenmore) on 16th June 1552.[6]

The Testament imagines the old robber's last farewell, reflecting upon his times among the inland glens.

Now fareweel Rannoch with thy loch and isle,

To me thou was richt traist baith even and morn.
Thou was the place that mad me not beguile
When I have been oft at the king's horn.

Fareweel Glenlochy with thy forest free;
Fareweel Fernay, that oft my friend has been;
Fareweel Morinch, alas, full woe is me!
Thou was the ground of all my woe and teen.
Fareweel Breadalbane and Loch Tay so sheen,
Fareweel Glenorchy and Glenlyon baith,
My death to you will be but little skaith.
Fareweel Glenalmond, garden of pleasance;
For mony fair flower have I fra ye tane;
Fareweel Strathbraan, and have remembrance
That thou shall never see Duncan again;
Atholl, Strathtay, of my death be fain,
For oft times I took your readiest gear,
Therefore for me see ye greet not ane tear.

* * *

At about this time Grey Colin evicted Gregor Dougalson of Balloch to build his own castle there. The Campbell policy of securing bonds of manrent was now continued into Breadalbane. Glenorchy's power was further increased when in 1554, the Earl of Argyll transferred to him the superiority of Glenstrae – an arrangement which was to be disastrous for the MacGregors.

Gregor Roy, the young heir to Glenstrae, was sent to fosterage with Sir Duncan Campbell of Glenlyon, known as Red Duncan the Hospitable of whom the priest would say at the time of his death: "To whose soul may God be gracious. He was not avaricious." (An unlikely epitaph for a Campbell in those times.) In 1502 Campbell of Glenorchy had bestowed a charter to Glenlyon to his second son Archibald, father of Red Duncan. The Campbell lairds had originally resided at Innerwick, until Red Duncan built a castle at Carnban (Carnbayne) where Gregor went to live.

Red Duncan may have favoured his young MacGregor foster son (his own son was mad) although there is a tradition that his wife, who was a Campbell of Lawers, hated the boy. In the event Gregor Roy married or eloped with Red Duncan's daughter, Marion Campbell and this love affair across their clans' divide added a singularly romantic aspect to the stories of his subsequent life as an outlaw.

In 1560, Gregor Roy came formally of age and so applied to Grey Colin of Glenorchy as his superior to confirm him in his tenancy of Glenstrae. But Grey Colin refused to do so – now clearly demonstrating the Campbells' policy to deny the MacGregors any feudal title.[7]

At the very start of his adulthood, Gregor Roy was thus made landless and faced with ruin. If he tried to possess his ancestral lands, the lowland law would issue Grey Colin with a writ of eviction, and the young MacGregor would have to comply or be denounced as an outlaw. Only one course was now open to him, and he gathered his clansmen to wage a personal war against Glenorchy. As well as the matter of his eviction, he inherited as chief a responsibility for exacting vengeance for the death of his old Tutor.

The Register of the Privy Council reported that the MacGregors "have massit themselves in great companies... and drawn to them the maist part of the broken men of the hale country, whilk at their pleasure burns and slays the poor lieges of this realm, reives and taks their guids, scorns and oppresses them and in sic sort that they are able to lay waste the hale bounds where they haunt and bring the samyn to be uninhabitable without the hastier remedie be providit therefore".

The "poor lieges" who were the targets of this raiding were for the most part Campbell settlers, and Gregor Roy received at least a tacit support from the other clans of the inland glens. The Privy Council went on to complain that "in all parts where they repair and haunt, they are reset (sheltered) by the inhabitants and indwellers thereof... and in sic wise fosterit and nourisit as gif they were the Queen's Majesty's true and faithful subjects and never had committed crime and offence in ony time bygane".

In fact, Mary Queen of Scots was strangely sympathetic towards the young MacGregor. Shortly after her arrival in Scotland, she visited Menzies of Weem (did she meet Gregor Roy there?) and learned from him about his impossible obligation to control the Gregarach, and possibly the causes of their disorder in the first place. She wrote to him from the lowlands shortly afterwards asking him "to permit them to occupy the same lands they had of you before, and make them reasonable taks there upon the usual terms and ye will do us thankful pleasure" – indicating thereby a shrewd grasp of the causes of the trouble.

Grey Colin of Glenorchy, however, was implacable in his pursuit of Gregor Roy. In 1563 he obtained from the lowland authorities a grant of all property belonging to Gregor Roy and his brothers "for the slaughter of Tearloch Campbell". The *Fortingall Chronicle* enters a brief notice of this fighting: "Ane guid simmer and guid harist, peace and rest except the laird of Glenorchy warreth against the Clan Gregor". Grey Colin was determined to follow the feud into the remoteness of Rannoch itself, and finding Menzies of Weem reluctant in this matter, offered to take the Gregarach problem off his hands. When Menzies (unwisely) accepted, Grey Colin brought in a warband of caterans recruited from the MacDonalds of Glencoe and Keppoch to drive the MacGregors out of their island stronghold and then threaten Menzies himself.

Again it was the Queen who intervened, and sent Grey Colin a private letter telling him to remove himself and his accomplices forthwith or legal writ would follow.[8] Grey Colin, however, used Campbell influence to persuade the Privy Council to provide him with Letters of Fire and Sword against the Clan Gregor in Perthshire and requiring all the other landlords in the area to render him assistance. Gregor Roy and his brother Ewin were formally pronounced outlaws.

But Grey Colin's abuse of these powers brought a barrage of complaints about his own head. The Earl of Atholl protested against the Commission of Fire and Sword and got himself exempted from its provisions. Colin's commission was summarily revoked. He was accused of using its powers indiscriminately to pursue his own interests against all his neighbours upon the excuse that they were helping the MacGregors – and had "nocht only allutterly abusit" his authority "bot als under colour thereof has by himself and other wicked persons his complices... committit sinsyne divers and sundry sornings, oppressions, herships, spulzies, yea and cruel slaughters upon divers our said Sovereign's lieges nocht being rebels". Grey Colin was thus revealed as being a principal instigator of disorder in the highlands, and his actions directed less at controlling the Gregarach than at suppressing his other neighbours in Breadalbane.

The Gregarach themselves had actually profited by this distraction by raiding further south into Menteith where the damage they accomplished was so great that the area was exempted from taxation until the next harvest could provide the wherewithal to pay. More ominously, there were, however, other signs of the Campbells' policy of manipulating the warring factions. There is record, for example, of the Earl of Argyll supporting Grey Colin with a bond to pursue Gregor Roy "to the death", and then afterwards (1563) employing the MacGregor chieftain to conduct a raid for the MacCailein's own purposes in return for a promise of pardon.[9]

In the meanwhile, a number of MacGregors who had signed bonds of manrent with Grey Colin, now repudiated them in favour of the chieftain of Glenstrae when Gregor Roy came of age, and this led to further reprisal and bloodshed. Two prominent MacGregors who returned to their clan allegiance were the sons of the Dean of Lismore who lived still at Fortingall at the mouth of Glenlyon. In 1565, almost certainly with the connivance of Grey Colin, a certain James MacGeStalkeir (The Son of the Hunter) went there in the night and murdered them both before setting fire to the house. The crime so horrified the government that a royal warrant was issued to the relatives of the dead men authorising them to pursue the murderers and excusing them from legal obligation to keep the peace during the execution of this duty. As clan chief, Gregor Roy took the responsibility upon himself, and catching up with MacGeStalkeir and his henchmen, he promptly put them to death. "They were wicked and oppressors of the poor and the said malefactors could not be suffered to live upon the earth."

Gregor Roy still appears to have enjoyed the favour of the Queen, who almost alone of her Council seems to have understood that the Campbell policy of evicting the clansmen without allowing them some alternative refuge was the direct cause of most disturbances in the highlands. "They cannot live without some rowmes and possessions", and she wrote again to Menzies of Weem requesting him to allow the Gregarach to dwell in Rannoch. She also issued a general pardon to the clan remitting all past offences.[10] Mary's dealing with the highland problem and with the MacGregors in particular provides a rare insight into her intelligence and sensitivity as well as her shrewd appreciation of what actually was going on. No other Stewart monarch before or after displayed such an understanding.

But by 1569, Mary was a prisoner in England and Grey Colin was free to move decisively against the MacGregors. He obtained a commission to take and execute Gregor Roy, and in May signed bonds with the Earl of Atholl and Campbell of Lawers to hunt him to the death. Menzies refused to sign, but Red Duncan of Glenlyon put his hand to the warrant.

Hunted up and down the length of Glenlyon, Gregor Roy was the first of the MacGregors to become the stuff of legend. His love for a Campbell bride lent the stories of his exploits a particularly romantic aspect. She is said to have been forced to return to her father's castle of Carnban, but Gregor Roy would elude the guards to visit her in the night. They were betrayed, by her mother perhaps, but Gregor escaped from the castle and eluded his pursuers by jumping the River Lyon at the place which is still called "MacGregor's Leap". Later, she is said to have joined him in the hills and they hid in a cave on the side of Schiehallion.

But eventually – inevitably – he was taken.

His trial was short since Grey Colin himself was judge, with the royal commission in his hand, and his power as Baillie of the district sufficient authority to order execution.[11]

"1570, the 7th day of April: Gregor MacGregor headed at Balloch."

The lament attributed to his widow is one of the most poignant pieces of Gaelic poetry:

> *Had there been twelve of his race and my Gregor at their head, my eyes would not be dim with tears, nor my child without a father.*
> *They laid his head upon an oaken block; they poured his blood on the ground; oh, had I a cup, I would drink of it my fill.*
> *Oh that my father had been sick, and Colin in the plague, and all the Campbells in Balloch in chains!*
> *I would put Grey Colin under lock, and Black Duncan in a dungeon…*
> *Oh that Finlarig were in flames, proud Taymouth lying in ashes, and Red Gregor of the White Hands in my arms again…*
> *Other men's wives sleep soft in their houses; I stand by the wayside wringing my hands.*

* * *

(Note: *Campbells of Glenlyon:* Carnban Castle was burned by raiders from Lochaber. Red Duncan was succeeded by his son Mad Colin who built Meggernie Castle but got a "clout on the head" and became unpredictable. Mad Colin's grandson left a widow who outlived three husbands at Meggernie. By a daughter of her second marriage to Patrick Roy MacGregor she was grandmother of the famous Rob Roy. The son of her first marriage was Robert Campbell who commanded the detachment that carried out the massacre of Glencoe. The daughter of her third marriage was also present at the massacre since she was married to the son of MacDonald of Glencoe. She escaped into the mountains.)

Campbells of Glenorchy

Sir Colin Campbell I (d.1480)
Duncan II (d.1513)
Colin III (d.1523)
Duncan IV (d.1536)
John V (d.1550)
Grey Colin VI (d.1583)
Black Duncan VII (d. 1631)
Colin VIII
Earls of Breadalbane

MacGregors of Glenstrae

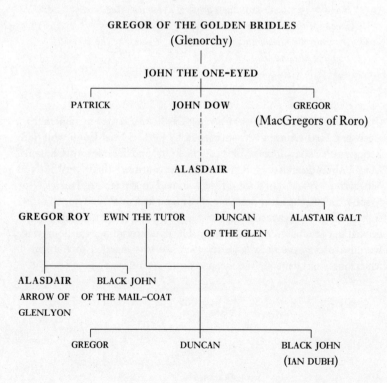

GREGOR OF THE GOLDEN BRIDLES
(Glenorchy)

JOHN THE ONE-EYED

PATRICK   JOHN DOW   GREGOR
(MacGregors of Roro)

ALASDAIR

GREGOR ROY   EWIN THE TUTOR   DUNCAN   ALASTAIR GALT
OF THE GLEN

ALASDAIR   BLACK JOHN
ARROW OF   OF THE MAIL-COAT
GLENLYON

GREGOR   DUNCAN   BLACK JOHN
(IAN DUBH)

CHAPTER 3

Alasdair MacGregor of Glenstrae – The Arrow of Glenlyon

Would I could see thee again in the hills of the deer,
With keen edged spear and hounds in leash following the chase;
Often the King of the forest fell to thy bow of yew –
Terror of all our foes, pride of Glenlyon!
Thou wert a skilled fletcher, thy quiver ever full.
See how the sharp arrow is winged with the eagle's plume,
Bound with silken thread, red and green from Ireland,
Waxed to shield the polished shaft from the heat of the sun.

Gregor Roy left two baby sons of whom the elder, Alasdair Roy, was barely three years old (the younger, later to be known as Black John the Mailcoat, may have been a posthumous child). The boys were put to fosterage with their uncle Ewin MacGregor, Gregor Roy's brother (who coincidentally was also married to their mother's sister, another daughter of Red Duncan called Mary Campbell of Glenlyon) and he became Captain of the clan and Tutor to Alasdair Roy during his minority.

The MacGregors took an immediate revenge for the death of Gregor Roy. Black Patrick, a surviving son of Duncan Ladasach, ambushed Grey Colin in Glenfalloch at the northern end of Loch Lomond and killed fourteen of the Campbells. He then led a major raid into Glenorchy and wasted that entire district, burning the steadings of the Campbell tenantry and lifting all their livestock.

However, after this immediate reprisal, the inveterate feuding of Gregor Roy's time appears to have almost ceased for some years – relative to the general condition of the highlands. Sporadic cattle raiding doubtlessly continued. Ewin the Tutor's two younger brothers, Duncan of the Glen and Alasdair Galt were summoned for poaching in the royal forests, and in 1581 Ewin with others was cited in connection with the death of a man called Duncan Stewart. But although the Privy Council would later refer

25

in retrospect to "the disobedience of the Clan Gregor and others broken men of the far Hielands... this twenty years bygane", the Register does not record any major incident or atrocity specifically attributed to the Gregarach for nearly fifteen years following the death of Gregor Roy.

This interlude may have been partly due to the prudence of Ewin the Tutor in obtaining the protection of Sir John Campbell of Cawdor "who had spent the most part of his time at court where he learnt all the subtilities thereof". Ewin and his brother Duncan of the Glen signed a bond with Cawdor agreeing to support his interests in all lawful affairs and not to act or permit others to act against him, while in the event of his own death, Ewin appointed Cawdor prospective guardian of his eldest son, Gregor. Cawdor enjoyed substantial power and influence with the government and was shortly afterwards appointed one of the guardians of the infant Earl of Argyll. He was therefore in a position to offer considerable protection to Ewin and his people.

The years of Alasdair's childhood were thus relatively trouble free for the clan. Besides his younger brother Ian Dubh (Black John) he grew up in the company of the Tutor's three sons – Gregor, Duncan, and another Ian Dubh. Their upbringing would have been in accordance with the circumstance and custom of the clan.

They had no schooling in the academic sense. Although he could speak English (with a Gaelic rather than a lowland accent), and although the MacGregors had traditionally respected men of learning such as the Dean of Lismore, Alasdair was illiterate and in later years was obliged to set his name to documents "with my hand touching the notary's pen because I cannot write". Illiteracy was no serious handicap to a highlander and it did not imply that a man was in any way dull-witted. However, for a chieftain who would have to pit his wits against the Campbell charter lords with all their lawyers' ways and clever men's deceit, it was likely to be a weakness. Alasdair in the tradition of his race, would put his trust in the spoken word – even of his enemies – and display thereby a fatal ingenuousness that would bring about his ruin.

The boys' education was practical, and in accordance with highland custom would have concentrated principally on the use of weapons and tracking skills. Young boys practised with single ash sticks until they were old enough to heft a full-size sword. Many highlanders still wielded the great claymores – two-handed weapons with a double-edged blade up to five feet in length – but there were also backswords and broadswords, and broad-bladed dirks worn at the belt beneath the plaid and used for close-quarter fighting held in the left hand with the point down. Some men also carried armpit knives called *sgian ockle* (stocking knives were not used since most clansmen went bare-legged).

Highlanders displayed considerable skill at swordsmanship acquired through disciplined and constant practice. Swords and dirks were the means of settling quarrels (fist fighting was regarded as a lowland custom) although a duel usually ended with honour satisfied when first blood was drawn. Young boys were therefore carefully trained in swordsmanship as an essential skill. Other favoured weapons were throwing spears, pikes, and Lochaber axes – a long-shafted axe with a hook on the end of it which was particularly effective against a mounted charge since horsemen could be gaffed out of their saddles like salmon in the spate.

A number of contemporary descriptions allow a glimpse of how highlanders looked and were seen at this time. Thus Nicolay D'Arfeville, Cosmographer to the King of France, writing in 1583:

> Those who inhabit Scotland to the south of the Grampian chain are tolerably civilised and obedient to the laws and speak the English language, but those who inhabit the north are more rude, homely and unruly, and for this reason are called savages (or Wild Scots). They wear like the Irish a full shirt covered with saffron, and over this a garment hanging to the knee of thick wool, after the manner of a cassock. They go with bare heads and allow their hair to grow very long and they wear neither stockings nor shoes, except some who have buskins made in a very old fashion which come as high as their knees. Their arms are a bow and arrow and some darts, which they throw with great dexterity, and a large sword with a single-edged dagger.[12]

The "cassock" referred to was the belted plaid worn by most clansmen. Contrary to previous and later custom, these were not multi-coloured tartans, but were generally reddish-brown in colour – the dyes extracted from tree bark (saffron only being imported) and Buchanan in his history of 1582 noted that highlanders understood the advantages of camouflage:

> They delight in variegated garments expecially striped and their favourite colours are purple and blue. Their ancestors wore plaids of many different colours and numbers still retain this custom, but the majority now in their dress prefer a dark brown, imitating nearly the leaves of the heather, that when lying upon the heath in the day, they may not be discovered by the appearance of their clothes...[13]

In battle the clansmen threw off their plaids and knotted their shirts between their legs. Clans distinguished one another by the badges usually worn on their bonnets – the MacGregors a sprig of pine, the Campbells the bog myrtle or fir club moss.

Hunting and tracking were other practical skills learned by young highlandmen. "Our delite and pleasure is not only in hunting of redd deer, wolfes, foxes and graies whereof we abounde and have great plentie" wrote a priest, John Elder to Henry VIII of England in 1543, "but also in rynninge, leapinge, swymminge, shootynge, and throwing of darts."[14]

The young Alasdair Roy won a particular reputation as a hunter, so that he was styled "The Arrow of Glenlyon" in the Gaelic praise poem dedicated to him as the chief. The region was heavily wooded and the ancient Caledonian forest teemed with game – red and roe deer, west of Loch Lomond the occasional wild boar, grouse and blackcock, swans, geese, ducks – to be killed for food; pine martens, wild cats, and on very rare occasions a wolf to be caught and skinned for pelts. Salmon and trout abounded in the lochs and rivers for the taking with nets or hazel rod and together with the other meats were an important element in the winter saltings.

In the outdoor months, the highlanders would range over prodigious distances, tracking deer (and stolen cattle), living simply off oatmeal and water, sleeping in the heather wrapped in their plaids, and learning an intimate navigation through the wild landscapes. As well as sport, it was a field training, tested in the *creach*, the cattle raid where a young chieftain could prove his leadership under campaign conditions, learn tactical planning and the use of ground – skills which were also needed to protect the clan's own cattle from neighbouring reivers.

Recreations included contests of strength, wrestling, putting the stone, tossing the *cabar* and competitive games like shinty which their ancestors had brought with them from Ireland, and a kind of unorganised football – in defiance of the lowland government which had "decreted and ordained that futeball be utterly cryit down and nocht usit" because it was considered a principal cause of riot.

The seasons dictated the patterns of highland life and custom. Spring, summer, autumn were the outdoor months, but the winters were particularly long and hard, with spring coming much later than it does today. Between 1550–1700 Scotland was gripped by the coldest weather since the Ice Age – in a climatic oscillation resulting from an expansion of the Arctic Ice Pack. In those times even the big inland lochs froze hard in winter, and come spring the earth itself took longer to thaw out. The lands deteriorated during this period, the harvests becoming gradually less plentiful.

Life centred on the herds of cattle, sheep and goats which were the clan's main currency, on the sowing and the harvest, and the need for winter fuel and food. The cattle at that time were a small shaggy aboriginal breed called *kyloes*, suited to the harsh terrain and bred for fattening and delivery to the lowland markets at the end of autumn. Inbyred or folded over winter they were often bled to make puddings of blood and oatmeal when the winter saltings ran low, and reduced also by lack of winter fodder, they had to be "lifted out" to pasture in the spring. The sheep were also indigenous and small, the fleece meagre but the wool long and fine for spinning or sale into the lowland and export trades. Goats provided milk, cheese, meat and skins.

Sowing took place in April. Arable land was worked in strips having been turned with a wooden plough or dug in lazybeds *(feannagan)* and fertilised with the accumulated winter cattle dung. Barley and flax were grown on the inbye land, and oats, the most important cereal were sown in the outfields[15].

For three weeks in May the men cut peat for drying before winter and then early in June the cattle were moved to the upland shielings where they spent the summer, thus allowing the grass on the lower pastures to recover. The beasts could be alternated between the two until the October sales. Stock to be kept over winter were held on the hill until the snows came.

In a good year, the barley and oats would ripen by September, and after harvest the clan would gather for the "Games". Women did the harvesting while the men went hunting deer or drove the cattle to the lowland markets (this was also prime cattle raiding time). They brought back the precious salt in which to preserve the meat and fish which would feed them through the winter. The peat blocks were brought down and piled outside the houses for the winter's fuel. Winter itself began at Martinmas (November).

It was a fragile economy when bad weather could mean a harvest ruined (which it was quite regularly) and the community struggling on the very edge of famine. In the wilder areas settled by the Gregarach it was existence on a primitive level, particularly in winter. In this situation a proscribed and landless clan would be vulnerable, and survival demanded a physical and mental vigour on the part of the young chief.

* * *

In 1583 there were signs that the period of truce – if truce there ever had been – was coming to an end. In that year, Grey Colin Campbell of

Glenorchy died and was succeeded by his son called Black Duncan with the Cowl *(Donacha Dubh nan Curich)*. Where Grey Colin had seemed implacable his successor would be relentless. If Grey Colin had been Clan Gregor's enemy, Black Duncan was to be their bane.

Energetic and ambitious, he began to consolidate the Campbell land throughout Breadalbane by building castles at Achallader, on the island in Loch Dochart, and Barcaldine in Benderloch. He improved the accessibility of Finlarig by constructing a bridge across the Lochay "to the great contentment and weal of the community". In estate management he introduced interventionist and lowland fashions of husbandry. He surrounded his houses with plantations of chestnut trees, with landscaped policies and gardens – and he enforced an old statute requiring his tenants also to plant trees around their cottages. He was a notable horse breeder and ran a herd of brood mares. He introduced fallow deer into his parklands (and, less wisely, rabbits).

Sophisticated for the age, literary and erudite, these things set him apart from the primitive highlandmen who bordered on his lands and threatened his property. The Gregarach he particularly despised, and a contemporary poem, making play with the MacGregor arms of a sword and pine tree crossed beneath a crown, has sometimes been attributed to his sarcastic mind – probably wrongly although the suggestion that a gibbet and a hangman's noose were a MacGregor's just deserts reflected his opinions accurately enough:

> *The sword and fir-tree crossit beneath ane croun*
> *Are fatal signs appropriate to his race,*
> *By some foreseeing fellow weel set doun,*
> *Meet for such limmers spoiling every place.*
> *The croun presents the King's most royal grace*
> *Ane richteous judge with skill wha does decree*
> *That they and all sic cut-throats should embrace*
> *His severe censure for their villainy,*
> *To wit, gif ony frae his sword goes free,*
> *Un-execute, continuing in their wrang,*
> *He will erect ane gallows of that tree,*
> *And thereupon in ane widdie hang.*
> *So far's my wits can serve, I can nocht ken*
> *Ane better badge for sic ane sort of men.*
>
> PS
> *One thing yet rests that suld their arms befit,*

*If with Sanct Johnstone's ribbons they were knit.**

* St Johnston's or Perth's "Ribbons" were hangman's ropes.

Black Duncan had already proved himself to have a treacherous disposition and his father Grey Colin had tried unsuccessfully to disinherit him. The more sinister aspect of his nature was perhaps revealed in the macabre collection of heading axes and instruments of torture which were listed in the inventory at Finlarig. From such an evil genius the Gregarach could expect little quarter.

At about this time also, that clan for their part seem to have returned to their marauding ways, possibly coinciding with the young Alasdair of Glenstrae making his bid for the leadership. In August 1586 Ewin the Tutor with Alasdair and 104 members of the clan were declared outlaws at Perth by Drummond of Drummond-Ernoch, the King's Keeper of the Royal Forest and Steward of Strathearn, in association with a number of other lairds in that district whose lands had been plundered. This suggests a raid in some force and may indeed have been the young chief proving his mettle.

In 1588, Alasdair Roy, like his father before him, formally applied to Black Duncan to be invested in his ancestral lands in Glenstrae. Like Grey Colin before him, Black Duncan absolutely refused, and when Alasdair tried to appeal to the Sheriff's court in Perth, the Campbell had the proceedings stopped. The old feud was in the open again, and Alasdair possibly started raiding into Glenorchy and harrassing the Campbell tenantry, since at about this time Black Duncan was granting tack of lands to "ones Donald and Dougal MacTearloch" (Campbells whose father had probably been killed by Gregor Roy) upon condition that they would:

> with the hale company and forces we may and can mak sall incontinent efter the date hereof enter into deidly feud with the Clan Gregor and sall continue therein and in making slaughter upon them and their adherents baith prively and openly and sall by nae manner of way nor persuasion leave the same... or cease therefra unto the time the said Duncan Campbell of Glenorchy find himself satisfyit with the slaughter we sall do and commit.[16]

This was a man determined upon the MacGregors' destruction.

In that same year (1588) there occurred an incident which was to lead to an atrocity that would cause great revulsion within the Privy Council and confirm in lowland minds that the Gregarach were no better than barbarous savages.

Some MacGregors in Balquidder were caught poaching deer in the royal forest of Glenartney by John Drummond of Drummond-Ernoch, the King's Keeper and Steward of Strathearn (the same who had two years previously denounced Alasdair and Ewin the Tutor as outlaws). Instead of holding them for trial, Drummond demonstrated the contempt for the Gregarach shared by people of his sort by cutting their ears off – to teach them and their kind a lesson. Among the Gaels, deer poaching was considered an honourable occupation for a free highland man (like cattle raiding) and when news of this foolish brutality spread around the clan, some act of revenge was predictable. The Privy Council on hearing of it were clearly alive to this danger since they required the Earl of Huntly (in whose jurisdiction the matter lay) to give a bond undertaking to keep Drummond under his protection.

In the autumn of 1589, Drummond was ordered to supply venison for the wedding celebrations of James VI and his Queen, Ann of Denmark. Somewhere in the forest he fell among a group of MacGregors who murdered him and cut off his head. In an act of quite wanton cruelty, they then called at the house of Stewart of Ardvorlich whose wife was Drummond's sister where they asked for food. When, in accordance with the rules of highland hospitality, she brought them bread and cheese to eat, they confronted her with her brother's head upon a platter, the mouth obscenely stuffed with the bread that she had served them, laughing that "he had eaten many a good meal in this house". The lady was pregnant and the horror sent her mad, so that for some days she wandered raving in the forest until her husband eventually found her and brought her home to be delivered of the child. (The baby boy to whom she gave birth was also to have a dark and troubled future.)[17]

These MacGregors had murdered the King's own Steward in the execution of his duty, and retribution was certain. Nevertheless, they did not attempt to hide the deed from their fellow clansmen, but carried the grisly trophy to the young chief of Glenstrae and asked for his protection. It was the custom among the Gaels, as among the early Celtic peoples, that a chief when inheriting responsibility for the welfare of his clan, adopted also the clan's enmities.

Alasdair, disposed perhaps by the fact that he was himself proscribed by the law, had been cheated out of his lands, denounced outlaw by the same late Drummond (who had clearly been hated by the clan), and motivated also by the desire to prove his leadership, now displayed a reckless defiance of the lowland authority by calling an assembly of the clan – not in the heart of the MacGregors' country but at the parish church of Balquidder near where the crime had been committed and arguably in the face of the Stewarts of Ardvorlich and others who had cause to seek revenge for Drummond's death.

The severed head was set on one of the gravestones, and laying his hand on it, Alasdair of Glenstrae swore to take the blood guilt upon his own head and not to surrender or reveal the murderers. He was followed in turn by the other clansmen in a remarkable but desperately foolhardy demonstration of solidarity and support for their young chief.

The reaction of the Privy Council was predictably drastic. On 3rd February 1590, after describing the action as "ethnic and barbarous" and "in maist proude contempt of our Sovereign Lord and his authoritie, and an evil example to other wicked lymmaris to do the like..." the Lords of the Council "being credibly informed of the cruel and mischievous proceedings of the wicked Clan Gregor, sa long continuing in blood, slaughters, herships, manifest reifs and strouths", outlawed the entire clan for the murder of Drummond-Ernoch. Alasdair of Glenstrae, his brother Black John, and his uncles Duncan of the Glen and Alasdair Galt with 135 members of the clan were specifically named together with "all others of the Clan Gregor or their assisters, culpable of the said odious murder, or of theft, reset of theft, hership and sorning."

Eighteen major highland landowners including the Earls of Huntly, Atholl and Argyll were commissioned to pursue and capture the malefactors dead or alive with powers to try and execute them on the spot – half of their possessions to go as a reward to the persons who apprehended them.

While Huntly and Atholl seem to have proceeded with an indifferent diligence, the Drummonds and the Stewarts were out to "take a sweet revenge for their cousin Drummond-Ernoch" and systematically hunted through the inland glens, The pursuit was also taken up by Black Duncan of Glenorchy who was the most active in executing his Commission of Fire and Sword. In August 1590 Black Duncan also applied for legal authority to eject Alasdair from Glenstrae.

The MacGregors under their young chief defended themselves vigorously, joining forces with other outlaw bands to raid in strength along the lowland fringe. This extensive reiving and burning caused widespread damage and disorder and the King angrily complained to his Council that "was nayther God nor man to comptroll and repres the defiance" of the wild highlanders. Alasdair himself continued to hold Glenstrae in the very face of Glenorchy's power.

Sporadic fighting and fruitless pursuit continued for a year. However, in addition to successful guerilla tactics and a desperate defence, the MacGregors also owed their survival at least in part to the influence of their principal protector, the old friend of Ewin the Tutor, Sir John Campbell of Cawdor.

CHAPTER 4

Black Duncan's Conspiracies

For close designs and crooked counsels fit,
Sagacious, bold, and turbulent of wit;
Restless, unfixed in principle and place,
In power unpleased, impatient in disgrace.

In September 1584, Colin, 6th Earl of Argyll died, leaving two small sons of whom the elder Archibald, was still a child of nine. With the prospect of controlling the vast Argyll estate over a long minority, the chief Campbell lords were quickly squabbling outside the nursery door.

The late Earl's testament had commended his heir together with his whole kin and friends to the "maintenance and protection" of the King. Principal charge of the young boy's affairs was left to the Countess his mother, who in turn was to have the advice and assistance of six "Guardians", namely: Sir John Campbell of Cawdor, Sir James Campbell of Ardkinglas, Sir Duncan Campbell of Glenorchy, Dougal Campbell of Auchinbreck, Archibald Campbell of Lochnell, and Neil Campbell, Bishop of Argyll.

However, of the six, the will provided that no important decisions could be taken affecting the young MacCailein Mor without the key signatures of Cawdor, Ardkinglas, and the Bishop – thus effectively concentrating power in the hands of these three.

This aroused the particular jealousy of Lochnell, who in the event of Argyll's direct line dying out, stood to inherit the earldom – a calculation which made him prey to uneasy ambition. It was also displeasing to Black Duncan of Glenorchy who had been on bad terms with the dead earl (complaining later as justification for his own behaviour "that his house had ever found greater friendship in other gentlemen than his chief") but "whose ambition and grasping character would not allow him to be satisfied with anything less than the entire control of the clan during the minority of the heir".

Black Duncan found in the susceptible Lochnell an easy tool to hand, and in 1584 the two signed a Bond agreeing to support each other "against all others, save only the King and their Chief". Cawdor countered by visiting Lochnell at his house in Lorne together with Ewin MacGregor, Tutor of Glenstrae, and somehow induced him to sign two papers wherein they in turn declared themselves dissatisfied with the young Argyll's guardians, agreeing to get the heir into their own hands and to support each others' interests. This may also have been intended to thwart Ardkinglas who had used his influence at court to procure the grant of the feudal right of ward and management of the young earl. However, after having been slighted by the Countess in some way, Lochnell reverted to Black Duncan of Glenorchy whose creature he then remained.

In 1588, Black Duncan exploited differences between Cawdor and Ardkinglas to draw the latter into a tripartite agreement with the Bishop – "knowing the upright mind and will that Sir Duncan Campbell of Glenorchy bore to the Earl of Argyll their chief and to his honour and the quietness of his subjects and country", and the other two undertook to "prefer the said Glenorchy to all others except the King and follow his counsel".[18]

The custom which allowed that at the time of pupilarity the young MacCailein Mor should nominate his own Guardians, occasioned a further change of partners in this complicated quadrille. Black Duncan and Campbell of Lochnell made their bid upon a proposal to associate themselves with the Earl of Montrose, the Earl of Loudoun (another Campbell) and Mr John Graham, Advocate. They were opposed by Cawdor and Ardkinglas who succeeded in procuring their own appointment together with the Earl of Mar, the Master of Glamis and Mr George Erskine, Advocate (Mar's brother). Cawdor therefore remained the major influence.

Cawdor and Ardkinglas thereafter fell out – apparently taking sides among other things in the clan feuds then disturbing the Western Isles (Cawdor putting up surety for MacDonald of Isla, and Ardkinglas for MacLean of Duart) – with each trying to procure the assassination of the other, until Ardkinglas died anyway in 1591. He was succeeded by his son, Sir John Campbell of Ardkinglas, a weak and vacillating man whom Cawdor quickly deprived of any power over the estate. The young Ardkinglas soon came under Black Duncan's influence (being married to his sister Annas) and would become later his incompetent accomplice.

This rivalry between Cawdor and Black Duncan acquired a further lethal dimension arising out of the murder of Drummond-Ernoch and Cawdor's subsequent protection of the Gregarach. Following the murder, Cawdor did little to execute his Commission of Fire and Sword against the outlaws; no more did Ardkinglas who was Alasdair of Glenstrae's cousin, and they gave shelter in Argyll to members of the Clan Gregor whom Black Duncan had hunted out of Breadalbane. This provoked Black Duncan to complain to the Privy Council in 1590 so that Cawdor and Ardkinglas were required to post security to aid him against the MacGregors on pain of being reported part of that clan. However, being themselves well connected at court, neither took any serious notice.

In August 1590, Alasdair of Glenstrae went raiding through the lands of Auchnafree belonging to Campbell of Lawers where he killed a few Campbells and then plundered Glenorchy's territory. Black Duncan, his brood mares slaughtered and his plantations burned, raised a picked force and pursued the MacGregors over the passes to their stronghold of Stronfernan in Rannoch. However, given word of his coming, the resident MacGregors under John Dow of Roro fled with their wives, cattle and goods to Blair Castle where the Baillie gave them shelter, and the Athollmen then joined them to repulse the Campbells and chase them back to Breadalbane.

Black Duncan again appealed to the Privy Council denouncing the gentlemen of Atholl and others for resetting (harbouring) the MacGregors. The Council were set to summon the Earl of Atholl to answer these charges when, upon Cawdor's personal intervention with the Chancellor, John Maitland, Lord Thirlestane, Black Duncan himself was abruptly summoned, cautioned to keep the King's peace and ordered to pay compensation to various people who had also complained about acts of violence which he had perpetrated against themselves and their property upon the excuse of legally persecuting the Gregarach.

If this was gall to Black Duncan's soul he was further tormented by a fresh order from the Council, also inspired by Cawdor, in December 1590:

> The King's Majesty with the advice of the Lords of Secret Council, grants and gives licence to Sir Duncan Campbell of Glenorchy, Knight, to contract, bond, enter into friendship and reconciliation of all bypast quarrels, deadly feuds, controversies and debates standing between him and the surname of MacGregor... and to the effect that the said friendship and reconciliation may be the more perfect, grants and consents also that such persons as the said Sir Duncan has presently in his custody, being friends, assisters and dependers upon the said Clan Gregor be put to liberty and freedom and suffered to pass where they please.[19]

Black Duncan was forced to comply, but when initial negotiations progressed only slowly, in July 1591 Cawdor again exerted his influence by setting a tryst between Black Duncan and the Gregarach at Kilchurn Castle "for composing of their variances"[20]. This resulted in the drafting of a formal Contract between Alasdair of Glenstrae and Black Duncan together with various other gentry under which both parties pledged themselves to abstain from robbery and mutual slaughter, and to keep their respective followers in order or be responsible for any further crimes committed by their dependants. This Contract was deposited in the official Register at Perth.[21] Six months later, in early January 1592, Alasdair MacGregor and his clansmen were given a government pardon for their part in the murder of Drummond-Ernoch and its aftermath, and were formally restored to the King's Grace as his "lovites".

While these negotiations were taking place inside Kilchurn Castle, Black Duncan left the meeting and took the young Ardkinglas for a walk among "the sauchen trees" at the head of the loch. The conversation that followed was recalled verbatim in Ardkinglas's later confession.[22]

Black Duncan began by reminding him of the distrust which had existed latterly between his late father and Sir John Campbell of Cawdor, and went on to complain bitterly about Cawdor's protection of the Clan Gregor despite the damage they had done to his own kinsman's lands about Glenorchy. If Cawdor were removed from the scene, he argued, "there is none worthy of his room but I. As for Lochnell, he is little guid worth, and as for the Bishop if he did not as we did we suld send him hame to his buiks". After that, said Black Duncan, "I and ye suld guide all efter our own will, and whatsomever commodity might be spyit out suld be equally parted between us baith."

When Ardkinglas nervously inquired just how the removal of Cawdor might be achieved, Black Duncan told him: "Cause some able young man to shoot him in his travelling or in a thack house where he usit commonly to lodge."

Ardkinglas, increasingly doubtful (as he later said) opined that they would be found out. "Why so?" answered Black Duncan. "If the man who shoots him shall escape after having done the deed you and I are not worthy to live if we cannot cut him away directly, and if he is presently slain we have the less adoe sae that nae man sall know who has done it – he having noe hand writ thereupon."

Later that day, when the meeting with the MacGregors had broken up, Black Duncan and Ardkinglas expanded on the plan as they rode together along Loch Aweside and over the pass to Inveraray where they were accomodated in "the old tower". During the night, after the somewhat risky fashion among conspirators in those days, they drew up a "Contract": "conforme to the communing we had upon the coich of Glenorchy anent the cutting away of Cawdor, the inbringing of (Sir Duncan Campbell of Glenorchy) to be my Lord Argyll's governor and the division of all commodities as is spoken in the 4th Article." Black Duncan wrote out a duplicate and both men kept a copy of the document. Since Black Duncan was too canny to do his own dirty work, it was left that Ardkinglas would find "an able young man" to carry out the murder – and arrange for the assassin to be suitably disposed of in his turn.

* * *

However, what Black Duncan did not tell the foolish Ardkinglas was that this was part of a much larger conspiracy relating to the wider political situation in Scotland and in particular to the close connection between the Earldoms of Argyll and Moray. In fact, Black Duncan and his associates were after bigger game than just Sir John Campbell of Cawdor.

The ancient Earldom of Moray dating back to the time of MacBeth and Thorfinn the Mighty [23] had ceased to be Celtic from the 12th century. King Robert I revived the title for his nephew Thomas Randolph, but on the failure of the male line it again reverted to the crown and was granted by Robert II to his son in law, John Dunbar. The last of the Dunbar earls was murdered in 1429, after which his daughter and her husband Archibald Douglas held the honour until it was forfeited on the occasion of his rebellion and death in 1455. Thereafter the earldom was bestowed on various scions of the Royal House until it was acquired in 1548 by George, 4th Earl of Huntly, head of the aggressively expansionist Gordon family, styled "Cock of the North", and, as Reformation loomed, leader of the Catholic party in Scotland. In 1561, the Earl of Huntly rose in rebellion against the Protestant Lords of the Congregation, but he was defeated and killed at the Battle of Corrichie, and the forfeited Eardom of Moray was next bestowed on the Queen's bastard brother, Lord James Stewart. When Mary was forced to abdicate, Moray became Regent of Scotland during the minority of James VI, but he was assassinated after four years leaving only two daughters and no male heir. His widow, Agnes Keith married as her second husband, Colin, 6th Earl of Argyll whose sister had married the lowland Lord Doune, and it was agreed that Doune's eldest son should marry the dead Regent's eldest daughter and thus inherit the Earldom of Moray. Young Doune became "the Bonnie Earl", having the Earl of Argyll for his uncle and the step-father of his wife.

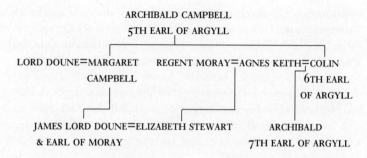

In 1590 the widowed Countess of Argyll remained close to her daughter and son in law of Moray, and Sir John Campbell of Cawdor as the principal among the young Argyll's guardians was active in the Argyll – Moray alliance. The new Earl of Moray, the young Argyll and Campbell of Cawdor thus inherited the enmity of George Gordon, 6th Earl of Huntly who hankered still after the Moray estates forfeited by his grandfather. This feud extended into the political sphere since Huntly was leader of the Catholic Party while Moray was the favourite of the Presbyterian faction – which during James VI's minority had been gaining the upper hand.

It extended also into the highlands, where, rather as the Campbells had developed a policy of acquisition among the ancient lands of the Gregarach, the Gordons although themselves a lowland family, pursued feudal claims among the territories of the Clan Chattan.

The Clan Chattan were originally a confederacy of clans claiming descent from Gilliechattan – "Servant of St Catan" (not dissimilar to the Siol Alpin) – made up mainly of the MacIntoshes, MacPhersons, MacBeans, Farquharsons and numerous cadets ranging through Lochaber, Badenoch, Braemar, Strathdearn, Moy and Inverness-shire. The chiefship was generally held by the MacIntoshes, an ancestor of whom had been seneschal of Badenoch under an early Comyn Lord, but who subsequently held land as tenants of Huntly as Lord of Badenoch (and, when Earl of Moray, their feudal superior). Just as Glenorchy had experienced with the MacGregors, Huntly discovered that the clansmen preferred their patriarchal chief to a feudal landlord, so that like the Campbells in Breadalbane, Gordon policy in the region was to create disunity among members of the highland confederation. Not surprisingly, the new Earl of Moray saw it in his own interests to support Huntly's highland opponents among the Clan Chattan.

In these circumstances Huntly wanted to deprive Moray of Argyll's (and that effectively meant Cawdor's) support, and was readily drawn into communication with Black Duncan of Glenorchy and Campbell of Lochnell. In addition to these three principals, a conspiracy was formed to include John Stewart of Appin (who was connected by marriage with Lochnell), John Lord Maxwell (who claimed the title of Earl of Morton), Duncan MacDougall of Dunnollie, Lachlan MacLean of Duart (whose ancestor had been murdered by Cawdor's grandfather and who resented Cawdor's support for MacDonald of Isla), and the Chancellor, Lord Thirlestane who, apart from the lands on offer, may have had some machiavellian design to influence the balance between the Catholic and Presbyterian factions. The historian Sir Robert Gordon averred that Thirlestane entered the intrigue "not so much for the favour he did bear unto Huntly as for the hatred he had conceived against the Earl of Moray... nor caring in the meantime what should become of Huntly or Moray, so he were rid of both."[24]

The plan was to procure the assassinations of the Earl of Moray, the Earl of Argyll, Colin Campbell of Lundy (Argyll's younger brother) and Sir John Campbell of Cawdor. The Earldom of Argyll was to pass to Campbell of Lochnell who was to reward his fellow conspirators out of its vast estates. Thirlestane was to to have Pinkerton in Stirlingshire; Black Duncan was to get Lochow and Benderloch; Stewart of Appin would be given the Earl of Argyll's lands within the old Lordship of Lorne, and MacDougall was to receive the lands of Loyng. It was intended that the murders should be carried out by highlanders and that Huntly, the Chancellor and Maxwell would engage to protect the others in the event of the plan's miscarriage.

Moray and Cawdor meanwhile were generally aware that Huntly was strengthening his position through bonds of manrent with the catholic Earl of Errol, Lord Spynie, Colquhoun of Luss, Menzies, Lochnell and Black Duncan of Glenorchy as well as some highland chiefs in the north west (notably Cameron of Lochiel) and so drew up their own contract with the Earl of Atholl, Lord Lovat, the Grants and others to counter the Gordon's alliance. Fighting broke out between the two factions in Morayshire.

In the latter part of 1590 there were in that district of Scotland musterings, marchings, and fightings, too obscure to make an appearance in general history, but enough to keep three counties in a state resembling civil war. Huntly, who acted as lord-lieutenant of the north and thus had a colour of law on his side, pursued the MacIntoshes and Grants who befriended the Earl of Moray, as rebels, both against himself, who was their feudal superior, and against the king. In a reconnoitring expedition which he made at Darnaway Castle, the Earl of Moray's house, one of his gentlemen was unfortunately killed by a musket-shot, discharged by a servant from the battlements – an injury which the feelings of the day made it a virtue to revenge.[25]

Following this incident at Darnaway, Lord Ochiltree, who was a friend of Moray, visited him at Doune and whether upon his own initiative or through external manipulation, persuaded him to travel to the House of Donibristle in Fife (which was owned by Moray's mother) where he hoped that it might be possible to arrange some reconciliation with Huntly. Moray, who trusted Ochiltree, accepted this advice and travelled to Donibristle with only a very small escort.

If Ochiltree had been sincere in attempting to broker some truce between Moray and Huntly, the latter had no such peaceful intention. At this juncture, a bizarre event of the previous summer provided Moray's enemies with the excuse they needed. In June 1590, Francis Stewart the (possibly mad) Earl of Bothwell, the King's own cousin, hereditary High Admiral, periodic outlaw, alleged warlock, and currently under indictment for abduction, necromancy and treason, had escaped from prison in Edinburgh Castle and in December of that year he attempted unsuccessfully to kidnap James VI from Holyrood House. Bothwell was also a cousin of Moray, and certain ill-disposed persons now put it about (almost certainly falsely) that Moray had been Bothwell's "inside" accomplice during the raid on Holyrood. This was used as grounds for serving Moray with a summons to appear before the Privy Council to answer these charges. His convenient presence at Donibristle would facilitate its delivery.

Precisely what instruction was given is not clear. According to one version of events, Huntly, acting on his own initiative, mustered forty mounted men and told people that they were headed for a horse race at Leith before turning back to Queensferry to cross the Forth into Fife. The most common account, however, is that James VI charged Huntly with bringing Moray to Edinburgh. Given the public enmity between them this would seem in retrospect to have been an extremely naive choice if there was any genuine intention to deliver Moray before the Privy Council undamaged or alive. Nevertheless James did issue an order stopping all ships leaving Queensferry that day (except for the boat carrying Huntly and his men) – possibly with a view to ensuring that Moray received neither help nor warning. Common gossip as repeated in a popular ballad of the day was that the Bonnie Earl of Moray was the Queen's lover, so that James might have had personal reasons for allowing Huntly this opportunity.

> *He was a braw gallant; he played at the glove*
> *And the Bonnie Earl of Moray he was the Queen's love*

On the night of 7th February 1592, Huntly's men surrounded the House of Donibristle and called on Moray to surrender. Moray had only Dunbar Sheriff of Moray and a few servants with him but refused to give himself up. The Gordons then gathered straw from neighbouring farms and piling it against the doors, set the house alight.

> The Earl of Moray, being within, wissed not whether to come out and be slain, or be burned quick; yet after avisement, this Dunbar says to my Lord of Moray: "I will go out at the gate before your lordship, and I am sure the people will charge on me, thinking me to be your lordship; sae, it being mirk under night, ye shall come out after me, and look if that ye can fend for yourself". In the meantime, this Dunbar came forth, and ran desperately amang the Earl of Huntly's folks, and they all ran upon him and presently slew him. During this broil with Dunbar, the Earl of Moray came running out at the gate of Donibristle, which stands beside the sea, and there sat down among the rocks. But unfortunately the said lord's knapscull tippet, whereon there was a silk string, had taken fire, which betrayed him to his enemies in the darkness of the night, himself not knowing the same. They came down on him on a sudden, and there most cruelly, without mercy, murdered him.[26]

The first dagger thrust is said to have been administered by Gordon of Gight, who turned next to Huntly and shouted "By God, my Lord, you shall be in this deep as I", whereupon Huntly slashed the Bonnie Earl across the face. "You have spoiled a better face than your own", Moray is alleged to have taunted him before dying of multiple stab wounds (and three bullets in his body as well).

News of the murder caused a popular outcry in Edinburgh. Moray's mother had his corpse carried in an open litter to Leith, "to be brought from thence to be buried in the aisle of the Great Kirk of Edinburgh in the Good Regent's tomb, and as some report to be made first a spectacle to the people at the Cross of Edinburgh; but they were stayed by command from the King." In fact, for propaganda purposes, Moray's body was kept above ground for some six weeks after his assassination, and the macabre painting of his naked and bleeding cadaver now hangs protected in the great hall of Darnaway Castle.

However, the government made slight pretence of bringing the murderers to book. Huntly was imprisoned for a little less than a month before being released. Blame was fixed upon Gordon of Gight who alone was hanged. In terms of the national political scene, if the Chancellor or James had hoped that Moray's removal might bring them some advantage over the Presbyterian faction, the plan misfired. From their pulpits the Presbyterian ministers made much of the murder and the derisory punishment meted to the perpetrators, and in the face of public opinion the Chancellor, whatever his own religious inclination, was forced to accomodate the Kirk. In June 1592, upon Thirlestane's advice, James was obliged to agree to the "Golden Act" – known as The Charter of the Presbytery – whereby King and Parliament confirmed all the liberties, privileges and immunities of the Kirk, whose government was given to its presbyteries, synods and the General Assembly, which had the right to meet as it wished in the presence of the King or his Commissioner. James VI's preference for episcopal government was thus severely prejudiced by his association with Moray's murder and its immediate aftermath. The Chancellor was also obliged to retire from court for a period due to the hostility of the Queen.

* * *

During the furore which followed the assassination of the Bonnie Earl, the murder of Sir John Campbell of Cawdor three days earlier (4th February 1592) had passed virtually unnoticed.

Since their pact at Inveraray, Black Duncan had not ceased to press Ardkinglas to fulfil his part of the scheme to encompass the death of Cawdor. Ardkinglas proved himself to be singularly inexpert at hiring assassins, but he eventually engaged a man called Gilliepatrick MacEllar whom he probably met through the agency of John Oig Campbell, a younger brother of Lochnell – an involvement of which Black Duncan, had he known of it, could hardly have approved. Since the contract killer also had no gun of his own, Ardkinglas lent him a "red-stocked hackbut" with which to carry out the deed. On the night of 4th February 1592, MacEllar crept up to the House of Knipoch in Lorne where Cawdor was staying, and shot him through the window. (In fact, he shot him three times, which given the time it would have taken to reload such a weapon, indicates a commendable conscientiousness on the murderer's part.)

But Ardkinglas now failed to complete the second part of the business – that is the disposal of MacEllar himself, who was helped to escape by MacDougall of Dunnollie. This did not please Black Duncan, since while MacEllar remained at large it was not safe to proceed against the young Earl of Argyll whose demise was the ultimate object of his design. He continued to press Ardkinglas to finish the business, but he now refused on the grounds that he counted MacEllar to be a personal friend. Black Duncan summoned him to Finlarig, and Ardkinglas's subsequent confession would indicate that there was a financial hold on him as well:

... he lying sick and I at his bedside, he usit the same language (that Ardkinglas should despatch MacEllar)... when I borrowed from him ane thousand marks for which he has my obligation and siller mark in pledge.

Realising that his young protégé was becoming a dangerous liability, Black Duncan decided to tell Ardkinglas that he was in too deep to withdraw now. One day at Dunoon, he again took him aside to "ane little green knowe whereon broom grows", where they sat together on the grass watching the young Argyll and some of his clansmen playing football. Black Duncan asked Ardkinglas if he had their earlier contract to murder Cawdor, and when he produced it (it seems remarkable that he should have kept such a document about his person) Black Duncan put it in his own pocket and refused to give it back.

He then acquainted Ardkinglas with the other contract between himself, Huntly, Lochnell and the rest engaging not only to murder Cawdor and Moray, but also the Earl of Argyll as well. Ardkinglas was horrified and absolutely refused to put his hand to it, whereupon Black Duncan lost his temper and told him that "he was unhappy ever to have to do with me or such a beast as I was."

Ardkinglas now became terrified that Argyll might suspect or even know about his complicity in the plot to kill him. In fact it is doubtful whether Argyll knew anything at this stage – although he had been aware of some kind of bond between Black Duncan and Huntly since he ordered his kinsman to withdraw from it – which Black Duncan ignored saying that "Bairns behovit to have fair words". But young as he still was (aged seventeen) Argyll was beginning to display a genetic disposition towards the ruthlessness and guile which would later earn for him the sobriquet of

Gillespie Grumach, or Archibald the Grim. Ardkinglas became convinced that Argyll did not like him, and in a state of self-generated panic he went to Margaret Campbell, the wife of John Oig Campbell who was held to be something of a spaewife, and asked her to intercede for him with certain witches of Lorne and "nowther to spare gowd nor gear to convert my Lord Argyll's anger and wrath in his (Ardkinglas's) favour." In the course of these transactions he confided to her the plot to kill Cawdor and her husband's own part in it.

Margaret Campbell immediately urged her husband to save himself by revealing all to the Earl of Argyll, but John Oig said that he could not betray his brother Campbell of Lochnell. Nevertheless rumours began to get about and in 1593, Argyll had learned enough to order the arrest of John Oig and Gillespie MacEllar. John Oig was put to the torture of the "Boot"and confessed to the part played by himself, Ardkinglas and MacDougall of Dunnollie in Cawdor's murder, but did not implicate Black Duncan or Lochnell. John Oig and MacEllar were condemned and hanged without further process.

Early in 1594 Argyll became seriously ill, and it was generally supposed that there was an attempt to poison him. However, he recovered and increasingly began to take charge over his own affairs. Ardkinglas and MacDougall were arrested and imprisoned, but probably through the influence of the Chancellor and Huntly, who obviously wished to suppress anything that might lead to the revelation of the wider conspiracy, they were not brought to trial. Ardkinglas was nevertheless held in custody for some time and in May 1594 a Commission was actually issued for his trial. Out of fear of being tortured or worse, he made a full confession of his plotting with Black Duncan, John Oig, and Gillespie MacEllar[27]. The episode involving the witches of Lorne was also corroborated by Margaret Campbell.

However, the Commission was revoked and Ardkinglas was eventually released. It seems likely that his confession was quietly suppressed by the Chancellor and others so that details did not reach Argyll's ears. Black Duncan was allowed to clear himself of all allegations by his own unsupported and extrajudicial denial – contained in a document dated 28th June 1594 signed at the Castle of Carrick in Cowal in the presence of the Earl of Mar, Hew Campbell of Loudoun, and Mr George Erskine, in which he offered to bide his trial (no doubt confident that the Chancellor and the other chief conspirators would prevent it).[28]

*   *   *

The murders of the Bonnie Earl of Moray and Sir John Campbell of Cawdor resulted in a fresh outbreak of disturbances in the northern and western highlands. In the North, the MacIntoshes and the Grants who had been Moray's supporters, began raiding into Huntly's territories in revenge for his death. Huntly retaliated by getting the Camerons to plunder the Clan Chattan's lands in Badenoch, while the Clanranald of Lochaber under MacDonald of Keppoch were similarly induced to harry the Grants along Strathspey. Keppoch seized the castle of Inverness but was driven out by MacIntosh (September 1593) who then held the town against Huntly and concluded an alliance with the Earl of Argyll. Huntly set himself to divide the Clan Chattan by pitting the MacPhersons angainst the MacIntoshes.

Meanwhile in Argyll, apart from the atmosphere of suspicion among the Campbell lords, the assassination of Cawdor caused a feud to break out between his relatives and the Stewarts of Appin. In the Western Isles, the truce secured by the sureties posted by Cawdor and the elder Ardkinglas broke down, leading in 1593 to summonses being executed against Angus MacDonald of Dunyveg, Donald Gorme of Sleat, John MacIan of Ardnamurchan and MacLean of Duart, for crimes of treason and lese majesty, and their forfeiture the following year set the context of the government's policy aimed at "the Danting of the Isles".[29]

In June 1594, a month after Ardkinglas's suppressed confession, the government learned (from Elizabeth I of England) of secret communications between the catholic Earls of Huntly, Errol and Angus and Philip II of Spain. Under heavy Presbyterian pressure, the King and Chancellor were forced to take action, and the three Earls were declared forfeited by Parliament.

Huntly and his associates gathered in arms, and the King issued a commission to the Earl of Argyll and Lord Forbes to proceed against them. Argyll raised a force of six or seven thousand men, mainly Campbells but also including Macleans, MacIntoshes, Grants, and interestingly a contingent of MacGregors, and laid siege to Huntly's Castle of Ruthven in Badenoch which was garrisoned by MacPhersons. Having failed to take it he marched over the hills to ravage the Gordon lands in Strathbogie, until approaching Glenlivat, he found Huntly and Errol astride his route with some fifteen hundred men – mainly cavalry but also with some highlanders from Clan Cameron and the Clanranald of Lochaber. Although advised to await the arrival of Lord Forbes who was approaching with further reinforcements, Argyll calculated that his force was strong enough and decided to offer battle.

One of the divisions in Argyll's force was commanded by Campbell of Lochnell who now saw another opportunity to arrange the death of his chief and his own succession to the Earldom. Accordingly he sent a secret message to Huntly telling him to attack the highlanders who would not withstand cavalry, and to concentrate his artillery on Argyll's banner. Huntly followed this advice, but miraculously Argyll survived the barrage and it was the luckless Lochnell who was struck by a cannon ball. Thus he inadvertently conspired to bring about his own destruction. Nevertheless Argyll's force was routed, to the young chief's bitter chagrin, although this was perhaps not altogether displeasing to the King who was wary of the Campbells' growing power and is said to have exclaimed: "Fair fa thee, Geordie (Huntly) for sending him hame a subject."

However, Huntly's advantage was of short duration since superior government forces quickly marched to pacify the north and demolish the castles of the insurgents. Huntly and Errol were forced to flee abroad, and Argyll took advantage of Huntly's enforced absence to secure for himself the manrents of MacDonald of Keppoch and Cameron of Lochiel – thus extending the Campbell power in the western highlands.

Black Duncan's conspiracies had come to an end, but he himself was not called to account. In 1596 he even managed to persuade Argyll to sign a bond with him promising to discredit all rumours spread by evil disposed persons against his "loving kinsman, Campbell of Glenorchy", and engaging to act kindly towards him and never misuse him in person or body.[30] As to what the MacCailein Mor really thought or knew, who then or later could fathom the Campbell's mind?

CHAPTER 5

Hostages to Fortune

Open was thy hand to thy friends
Ever the ready smile to greet clansman or chieftain;
None ever left thy threshold with a heavy heart.
Strangers came from afar, and the harpers of Ireland sang,
To the tunes of old days, the praise of thy deeds in war.
They drained the wine cup, the pipes' merry music rang –
Alas, are those bright days gone forever?

Cawdor's assassination occurred barely a month after the official pardon given to Alasdair of Glenstrae and his followers for the murder of Drummond-Ernoch and their subsequent behaviour. Moreover, since the pardon had only been granted as a favour to Cawdor, following his death some people were quick to question its validity. The Stewarts of Ardvorlich in particular remained intent upon revenge, and intermittent fighting continued between them and the MacGregors around Balquhidder. This gave the government sufficient excuse to issue new Letters of Fire and Sword, and while as before, some like Argyll were not diligent in enforcing them, others – notably Galbraith of Culcreuch and the Buchanans – were ready to purchase commissions that allowed them to pursue feuds of their own under the pretext of lawfully persecuting the Gregarach.

In fact, their particular targets were Aulay MacAulay of Ardincaple in the Lennox, and his neighbour, Colquhoun of Luss. MacAulay complained to the Privy Council that Galbraith and Buchanan "under colour of searching and seeking for the Clan Gregor" had used the authority of the Letters of Fire and Sword "to assiege (his) houses and raise fire therein; whereof (Galbraith) has already given sufficient proof, by the convocating of the hale name of Buchanan for the maist part in arms, with whom the said MacAulay stands under deidly feud". The Buchanans, claimed MacAulay, had on one occasion cut down two of his men, while he himself had barely escaped with his life. For his part he denied helping the Clan Gregor.

MacAulay had the support of the Duke of Lennox, and the government cancelled the Letters of Fire and Sword. However, MacAulay had been somewhat sparing of the truth. The MacAulays were an old offshoot of the Clan Gregor, and in 1591, while Alasdair of Glenstrae was still outlawed, Aulay MacAulay had signed a Bond of Manrent with him acknowledging Alasdair as his chief and promising him his *calp*, while Alasdair for his part, had promised to "fortify, maintain, and assist the said Aulay MacAulay, his kin and friends, in all their honest actions against whatsoever person or persons, the King's Majesty only excepted." It is unlikely that the Privy Council were aware of this agreement, but they did take securities from MacAulay not to "reset" the Clan Gregor.[31]

This relationship with MacAulay provided Alasdair of Glenstrae with some temporary relief but it complicated his situation in the long term.

* * *

King James VI meanwhile, had decided to take a personal interest in the "improvement of the Highlands". Ever since the slaughter at Harlaw, highland disorder had been a constant preoccupation of successive Stewart kings. James I, who had prayed that "If God gives me but a dog's life, I will make the key keep the castle and the bracken bush the cow throughout all of Scotland", had displayed a particular contempt for the Gaelic clans, and enforced violent justice by the sword and hangman's rope. But while he executed numbers and humbled Alexander of the Isles, the submission was not permanent. In James IV's reign, the forfeiture of the Lordship of the Isles, far from establishing the influence of the lowland government, had the effect of destabilising the Western Isles by removing the principal focus of authority so that the vassal clans were left unchecked to pursue their individual quarrels and policies of territorial aggrandisement.

> The Islanders and the rest of the Highlanders were let loose, and began to shed each other's blood. Although the MacDonald kept them in obedience while he was Lord over them, yet upon his resignation of his rights – all families including his own as well as others, gave themselves up to all sorts of cruelties which continued for a long time thereafter.[32]

Of all the Kings who had attempted to bring order to the Highlands, James VI was the most unlikely, and yet probably the most successful. The methods were peculiar to himself and his nature of government – the combination of law and its enforcement, an exploitation of the charter lords' own ambition and greed, a mixture of temporising with punishment, justice with arbitrary injustice. Moreover, as much as the King hated disorder he was the more practically driven by financial considerations, and particularly the need to replenish an exchequer which he had himself drained largely by his own extravagance and prodigality.

In 1587 the Scottish Parliament had passed the General Band which principally enacted that all landlords in the Borders and Highland regions had to assume legal responsibiloity for the behaviour of their followers and dependants. If any of these should be accused of a crime, the landlord was obliged either to produce the alleged offender to answer the charge or pay the damages himself, while the Band authorised reprisals against any member of the criminal's clan if the actual culprit was not brought to justice.

However, no landlord or feudal superior would voluntarily assume responsibility for broken men. Such were therefore declared under the Band to be deemed followers of the landlord on whose territory they were settled or even living temporarily, and these landlords had either to accept resposibility or evict them. Chiefs of clans considered to be habitually disorderly were to give hostages for the good behaviour of themselves and their clansmen. A list of Highland and Border landlords was appended to the Act but it did not contain the name of MacGregor since the Gregarach had no landlord to represent them. Instead, they were included in a second list of clans which were deemed to have "Captains, Chiefs and Chieftains whom on they depend, oft-times against the will of their landlords".[33]

Further legislation in 1593 confirmed the obligation of landlords and baillies to find sureties for their duty to apprehend offenders living under their jurisdiction and to make reparation for any injuries committed by such persons, failing which an injured party was entitled to proceed at law against the sureties for the amount of damage sustained. In addition to this obligation to reimburse his sureties, the landlord could also incur a heavy fine to the Crown. In the case of "broken clans" such as the MacGregors, dwelling on the properties of various landlords but depending on their own clan chiefs, these obligations of arrest and reparation were also to rest on those chiefs, who in addition had to produce hostages as pledges for their obedience, and to relieve these hostages on a quarterly basis – failing which they would be declared public enemies "to be perseuit with fire and sword".

This meant that a chief who was himself a feudal superior could deal with crimes committed within his own area of jurisdiction. However, the chief of a "broken clan" such as the Gregarach would be obliged to surrender an offender for trial – which was unlikely to be acceptable to the clan. Nor, while clansmen were ready to stand hostage for their chief, were they as willing to be hostage for the behaviour of each other.

After the death of the Chancellor Thirlestane, James VI increasingly took highland matters into his own hands, and the financial motive became more apparent. In 1597, a further Act made it imperative upon all land-lords, chieftains and leaders of clans, and others possessing any right to land, to produce their title deeds before the Lords of the Exchequer on 15th May 1598. The preamble to this Act stated that the Highlanders had not only neglected to pay the yearly rents and other services due to the Crown, but through their "barbarous inhumanitie" they had made the fertile highlands and islands altogether unprofitable so that honest merchants could not trade with them in peace or safety. The Act there-fore provided also that chiefs had to post security for the regular payment of rents and for the peaceable and orderly behaviour of those for whom under the law they were bound to answer. The penalty for disobedience was the absolute forfeiture of all title to their land.

Given the fact that many highland landlords had probably lost their title deeds – if they ever had any at all – and the difficulty in finding the requi-site security or bail, James VI probably intended that large tracts of land would be acquired by the Crown – with consequent opportunity for him to embark on his other schemes for the "improvement of the Isles".

* * *

Alasdair of Glenstrae had been giving thought as to how he might find another powerful "protector" to take the place of the murdered Campbell of Cawdor. The persecution of the MacGregors following the incident of Drummond-Ernoch's head had taught him caution and a more mature recognition that his responsibilities were not so much to the wilder spirits among his clan – the grandsons of Duncan Ladasach and their like – as to "the poor innocent men and young bairns", and the more defenceless of the evicted families who were truly dependent upon him as their patri-monial chief.

MacAulay had won him some respite against Galbraith and the Buchanans, but the latest government legislation became the occasion for further widespread evictions. Landlords who found it expensive enough to have to answer for their own clansmen and legal tenants, were not willing to take responsibility for the behaviour of "broken men" so notorious as the Gregarach. Even landlords previously sympathetic towards them declined to take the risk, and Menzies of that Ilk now applied for a writ to eject Alasdair of Glenstrae "pretendit tenant and occupier of thirty two merkland of Rannoch".

Their old enemy, Black Duncan with the Cowl, had particular reason to evict Alasdair's people and absolutely refused to be held liable for the behaviour of outlawed cattle thieves. Having failed to eject Alasdair by force, he complained again to the Privy Council that he ought not to be held accountable for the MacGregor – who had actually been declared at the horn for not evacuating "fra the said Sir Duncan's lands of Stronmelochan and their pertinents, and because he remainit at the said process of horn still possessit and occupiet of the said Sir Dincan's lands by violence agains his will, as he does yet notwithstanding that Sir Duncan by his proceedings against the said Alasdair has followit out the order proscrivit by the General Band anent the removing of broken men fra lands who are not answerable". Black Duncan was consequently excused responsibility for the MacGregors, but Alasdair was considered an outlaw again.[35]

In the face of Black Duncan's implacable hostility, Campbell politics encouraged Alasdair to believe that the Earl of Argyll himself might be a possible counterweight and provide the protection which he needed. Messages exchanged through third parties indicated that Argyll would be ready to consider some arrangement.

But needless to say, Argyll had his price. It was the old one – that Glenstrae should lend MacGregor caterans to harrass the Campbell's neighbours. Argyll had two victims particularly in mind: – Ardkinglas of whom he may have suspected many things, and Aulay MacAulay whom he associated with the interests of the Duke of Lennox. (Argyll was at that time in dispute with Lennox over the office of Admiral of the Western Seas, which carried with it the lucrative rights to collect excise duty on all the herring landed at western harbours.)

Both posed problems so far as Alasdair's honour was concerned: – Ardkinglas because he was kin "and the man I did maist trust unto" (which says much for his sense of highland loyalty but little for his judgement of men), while MacAulay had offered him his *calp*, thus acknowledging him as chief with all the reponsibility attached to his acceptance of the manrent, and had helped him against the predations of Galbraith and the Buchanans. Glenstrae could not therefore accept Argyll's terms.

In this dangerous quandary, Alasdair resolved on the daring alternative of going to court and putting his case directly to the King. He was illiterate and probably uncouth by lowland standards, but the young highlander was prepossessing and would be something of a novelty – and James VI was known to be susceptible to both. The King was also a keen huntsman, and the "Arrow of Glenlyon" had few equals with a bow. Accordingly, in July 1596, he went to Dunfermline and threw himself upon the kindness of the King.

He entered the royal presence "in maist humble manner, acknowledging his offences and disobedient past whereof he maist earnestly repented" and pledged himself to maintain order among his clan thereafter for which he would be responsible to the King and his justice. It was decided that he should be held as a hostage, but not strictly under arrest – being required to remain within the King's household, forbidden to leave without the King's personal and written authority, and to swear an oath to be faithful "as the King's household man… as he would answer to God upon the salvation of his saul".

This initiative was in the short term at least more successful than Alasdair might have hoped, since he was given a new and sweeping pardon, acquitting him and his followers of the murder of Drummond-Ernoch and "for all other (crimes) committed by the said Alasdair or by any other of the surname of MacGregor".[35]

Nothing is known, however, of how otherwise he fared at court or with the King. In 1597 he was back in the Highlands – possibly trying to make good the pledges which he had given.These proved virtually impossible to fulfil. Under the General Band he had to post bail for himself and his clan. The amount asked for was as high as 10,000 or even 20,000 merks – sums which he could not hope to raise, even for his own caution. Nor would others lend such sums as surety for the behaviour of a clan with the reputation of the Gregarach. He was able to settle some of the more peaceable of his folk under other landlords, but the majority of his clansmen remained his own responsibility, and the wilder spirits were not amenable to control.

His own closest relations were among the worst. Ian Dubh nan Lurach, his brother and the Tanister of the Clan Gregor, who had married a Murray of Strowan and settled in Balquhidder, had reached his own accomodation with the Earl of Argyll and raided through Strathbraan and along Tayside. The other Black John, son of Ewin the Tutor (Ian Dubh MacEwin) together with his two uncles, Duncan of the Glen and Alasdair Galt refused to recognise the conditions of the General Band and also returned to their old ways so that their reiving in Glenorchy provoked fresh complaints from Black Duncan and another declaration of outlawry. Other clansmen such as John Galt MacGregor who was regularly cited for a variety of offences, regarded themselves as professional thieves anyway and could not be disciplined.

Nevertheless, it does appear that Alasdair did everything he could to keep his clan at peace, so that apart from the endemic cattle lifting, they were not otherwise accused of any serious bloodshed during the decade 1592–1602. However, continual cattle theft, even on a relatively small scale, kept the bad reputation of the clan in the forefront of lowland prejudice.

This rendered the MacGregors vulnerable in their turn to other highland aggressors, incited quite possibly by charter lords of mutual acquaintance. In 1598 a band of MacLeans from Mull raided through Rannoch and plundered the MacGregors who were settled there. Instead of striking back in force, which would have been the highland way, Alasdair took the quite extraordinary step of indicting MacLean of Duart before the High Court of Justiciary in Edinburgh – the first time a chief of the Clan Gregor had ever "come and sought justice... sin James I". MacLean was ordered to pay compensation, but merely scoffed at the sentence. The MacGregors of Rannoch who eked a precarious subsistence from the land were further impoverished by the MacLeans' raid. Starvation threatened. The fat lands of Glenorchy and the Lennox beckoned. Argyll's offer was still open.

The temptation must have been great indeed and the pressure to conclude a deal with Argyll enormous. But Alasdair knew Argyll to be the instigator of his troubles. "Sin I was first his Majesty's man", he later dictated in his confession, "I never could be at ane ease, by my Lord of Argyll's falsheid and inventions; for he causit MacLean and (Clan Cameron) to commit hership and slaughter in my rowme of Rannoch, the whilk causit my puir men thereafter to beg and steal".[36]

So Alasdair continued to resist Argyll. In 1599, he again appeared before the Privy Council to answer for the misdemeanours of his clan. The government now began to recognise the hopelessness of his situation and the need for some practical solution, since with the co-operation of John Murray of Tullibardine (one of whose clanswomen was married to Ian Dubh), together with the Commendator of Inchaffray and even of Black Duncan of Glenorchy (who may have seen it as a less expensive alternative to the constant cattle raiding) the Privy Council accepted a working arrangement proposed by Alasdair himself.

Because it is impossible to the said Alasdair to find inland caution upon the conditions of the General Band... in respect neither is he responsall in the sums whereupon the caution is founden, and that nae inland man will be caution for him in respect of the bypast enormities of his clan, therefore it is offerit that the said Alasdair, for satisfaction of His Majesty's honour sall come in his Highness will for any offence committit by himself, and he sall deliver to His Majesty three pledges (hostages) to be namit by His Majesty out of the three houses of that clan – John Dubh MacGregor being always exceptit, to be placit where His Majesty and Council sall appoint, to remain as pledges for the guid rule and obedience of the hale clan and name of MacGregor; and for such of the said clan as be inobedient, he sall either enter them to His Highness or his Justice or else use justice on them himself, he having His Majesty's commission to that effect.[37]

Thus Alasdair swore to be responsible for all the people of his clan whom he could not settle under other landlords, while for his own part, he agreed to "come in His Highness' will" – meaning that the King could decide upon any punishment to be meted out to him without the formality of trial in a court of law.

Tullibardine and the Commendator of Inchaffray declared that they were willing to be "cautioners" for Alasdair under this agreement, and swore to produce him and the first of the hostages before the Council on the 4th September following (1599). They duly appeared on that date and handed over Ian Dubh MacEwin – but made excuses for Alasdair who they said was "visite with infirmity and sickness sae that he was not able to travel".

Alasdair's appearance was formally postponed until November, and then again until 29th January 1600. However, on that day, when neither hostages nor cautioners reported at the appointed place and time, the Council fined the cautioners 10,000 merks for not producing Alasdair and a further 5,000 merks for the absence of Ian Dubh MacEwin. The Council also denounced Alasdair as having "maist undutifully and unhonestly violated his promise" and threatened to prosecute the Clan Gregor "with all rigour and extremitie".

Tullibardine explained somewhat elliptically that Alasdair's absence was due to "some occasions whilk intervenit and fell out before the day of his entry, whilks discouragert and terrifiet him to keep the first diet". By this he was referring to his knowledge that Alasdair had again been approached by the Earl of Argyll who persuaded him that the Privy Council intended some trick.

I made my moyan to please His Majesty and Lords of Council baith of service and obedience both to to punish faltours and to safe innocent men. And when Argyll was made foreseen thereof, he entisit me to stay and start frae thae conditions causing me to understand that I was deceived; but with fair words to put me in ane snare... began to put at me and my kin.[38]

In this, Alasdair was displaying an ingenuousness and political naiveté which would ultimately prove fatal.

Confronted with having to pay 15,000 merks, Tullibardine promptly delivered Alasdair in Edinburgh with a deal of eloquent explanation and excuse. He was pardoned and relieved of the fine. But Alasdair was imprisoned in Edinburgh Castle.

On 6th March 1600 the Privy Council convened a conference of all the landlords upon whose lands the MacGregors were camped to debate what should be done. Discussion centred on the common complaint that the main reason for "the misrule and disobedience of that clan and the inability of the landlords to make them answerable" was "the reset and comfort whilk they fand of their said chief and amongs the landlords themselves, seeing that every one of them for the most part reset the men and tenants of others, when they were pursuit by their maisters or when they had committed only wicked or evil deeds". This was probably an accurate diagnosis. So each blamed the others – and all blamed Alasdair.

In this continuing impasse the Privy Council could not think of any substantive improvement to the working arrangement agreed with Tullibardine the previous autumn. It advised that each landlord should take responsibility for as many MacGregor tenants as he was willing to acknowledge, while Alasdair of Glenstrae was to be personally accountable for the rest. In the meanwhile he was to remain in Edinburgh until the three hostages should be delivered to the Privy Council.

At the beginning of April 1600 this arrangement seemed to have been satisfactorily concluded when the three hostages duly surrendered themselves, allowing Alasdair to return to Glenstrae. As loyal clansmen it was their duty to ransom the body of their chief. However this loyalty and sentiment did not necessarily extend to their fellows of a lesser standing – as subsequent developments would show. Nor was Archibald the Grim, Earl of Argyll, likely to rest content.

CHAPTER 6

The Slaughter at Glenfruin

Proudly our pibroch has thrilled in Glenfruin,
And Bannochar groans to our slogan replied:
Glen Luss and Rossdhu, they are smoking in ruin,
And the best of Loch Lomond lie dead on her side.

Archibald the Grim – Gillespie Grumach – Earl of Argyll, was now in his early twenties and demonstrating the disposition which earned him that name. He displayed a particular hatred towards Campbell of Ardkinglas whom he hounded out of his lands. Campbell clansmen led by a bastard son of the murdered Cawdor attacked Ardkinglas's house, robbed and beat his servants, and abused his wife. Argyll seized his lands and, as Ardkinglas vainly complained to the Privy Council, "violently debarrit him therefra". Then as if determined to break him utterly, he persuaded the government to order him to post caution under the General Band for 10,000 merks – a sum which, deprived of his lands and the income therefrom, he could by no means find. Nor, complained Ardkinglas, should he have been compelled to do so, since all his people were sub-tenants of Argyll who was therefore their accountable superior – an argument to which the Earl remained impervious.

He also pursued a violent feud against Aulay MacAulay. Campbell bands led by Argyll's lieutenants – Duncan Campbell the Captain of Carrick, and Neil Campbell of Lochgoilhead (known as Neil the Traitor) – raided his estates, burned his houses and plundered his tenants. They laid ambushes for MacAulay and in an incident reminiscent of Cawdor's murder, attempted to assassinate him at his house in Greenock by firing through the window. MacAulay was shot in the body but survived.

The instigation of this violence was directly attributable to Argyll, who did not bother to deny it and even signed a bond acknowledging that the guilty parties were "his proper men and servants" and thus his legal responsibility under the General Band. However, he took no action to restrain them or bring them to justice (he being also Justiciar of Scotland). Nevertheless, the fact that he was obliged to employ his own clansmen and so reveal his involvement was an inconvenience, when the use of surrogates such as the MacGregors would have provided some measure of deniability. He therefore continued to put pressure on Alasdair of Glenstrae.

> He did all his crafty diligence to entice me to slay and destroy the laird Ardincaple, MacAulay, for ony gains, kindness or friendship that he might do or give me. The whilk I did refuse in respect of my faithful promise made to MacAulay of before. Also he did all the diligence he could, to move me to slay the laird of Ardkinglas in like manner; but I never grantit thereto; through the whilk he did envy me grettumly.[39]

But events, together with Alasdair's own desperate situation eventually played into Argyll's hands.

In the autumn of 1600, Alasdair was obliged to replace the hostages for Clan Gregor who had been surrendered to the Privy Council during the spring. These are recorded as having been John MacIanduy and Ewen MacAlasdair Pudrach placed in the custody of Murray of Tullibardine, and John Patrick Vic Ian consigned, perhaps ominously, to the keeping of Black Duncan of Glenorchy. But while these had willingly surrendered themselves to ransom the person of Glenstrae as their chief, no volunteers appeared to take their places when the agreement required that they should be relieved.

In March 1601, the Privy Council once again formally declared Alasdair an outlaw for failing to produce fresh hostages, due to "the perverse counsel and inclination of his wicked and misrulit clan", and for clearly demonstrating by this that far from intending to keep to the agreement, he had proved ready to "oversee and wink at the insolences and attempts of the disorderit thieves and limmers for whom he ought to answer".[40]

It was a significant coincidence that the Earl of Argyll was sworn in as a Privy Councillor at the same meeting, and that the Council then passed a resolution to the effect that the King, being desirous of having "the said insolent limmers repressit and reduced to obedience" formally appointed Argyll, whose "guid inclination" particularly fitted him for this commission. To this end he was given authority to summon the Clan Gregor and take sureties from them, with power also to "prosecute them as fugitives and outlaws with fire and sword, and to burn their houses, and to follow and pursue them wherever they shall flee... and to raise fire and use all force and engine which can be had..." He was also given the power to summon their landlords to produce them under the General Band and to convene justice-courts to try and convict them as he should decide. More draconian still, the Privy Council further allowed that, in order that he might not be constrained in the exercise of his commission, the Crown waived all rights to interfere in his decisions or to grant mercy to those MacGregors whom he might condemn. The commission was even made retrospective to 1596. This effectively gave him absolute control over the destiny of the Gregarach. However, as his neighbours were soon to discover he had no immediate intention of condemning anyone who could be useful and would do as they were told – and Argyll had his own plans for the Clan Gregor.[41]

For his part, Alasdair of Glenstrae could resist no longer. The winter had been particularly cold and many of his people were starving. Moreover for many of them Argyll's proposals were extremely agreeable and the thought of raiding into the Lennox under his protection was most congenial to men such as Ian Dubh (John of the Mail-coat – Alasdair's brother) and the fierce sons of Ewin the Tutor.

To enforce his authority Argyll ordered Alasdair to appear before his first justice-court in Stirling on 22nd April 1601. Glenstrae's former obligations to the Privy Council were formally transferred to Argyll, and Alasdair undertook to account for his clan's actions and to deliver hostages under pain of "the loss of his lands to the said Earl forever". He himself was to remain in custody until he had paid all damages due on claims for injury presented to the court before 12th May. (Black Duncan of Glenorchy took advantage of his absence to burn Alasdair's house at Stronmelochan and drive the last of the MacGregors out of Glenstrae – subsequently obtaining a remission for this violence.) The terms of the agreement were incorporated in a document to which Alasdair was obliged to attest, "with my hand touching the notary's pen underwritten because I cannot write".[42]

But Argyll had no inclination to impose law and order on the Gregarach, as his neighbours soon discovered to their cost. Complaints to the Privy Council resulted in a summons to Argyll to appear on 3rd August 1602 to account for the implemetation of his commission – or rather his failure to implement it. He did not appear, and when he was then denounced as being a rebel himself and fined 20,000 merks (the surety which he had given), he did not pay. The Council complained that he had completely failed to control the MacGregors who were "als insolent and of als unhappy and mischievous a disposition als they were at ony time preceding, and has committed open and avowit herships and depredations upon fair day light". Yet Argyll himself was most probably the instigator of these "herships", and lowland law was subordinate to Campbell order among the inland glens.

The Gregarach happily reverted to their old ways, raiding into the fat lands of the Lennox with Argyll's licence to despoil his enemies and reset their booty among his friends. Highland honour still forbade them to damage Ardkinglas or MacAulay, but Argyll had other neighbours to whom the MacGregors were not attached (or with whom they were in fact at feud themselves) where constraints of kinship did not apply and who could be considered as fair prey. Among such was the Roman Catholic Earl of Airlie whose highland estates stretched from the Braes of Angus to the boundaries of Perthshire and Aberdeen, and 200 clansmen, mainly MacGregors, raided deep into Glenisla and lifted a hundred horse and countless cattle.

Another of Argyll's neighbours and the target of his choosing was Colquhoun of Luss.

* * *

The Colquhouns were a surviving branch of the ancient rulers of Lennox – originally a saintly family, Celtic priests and hereditary guardians of the crozier of St Kessog, the martyr who was said to have dwelt in Glenluss or at Inchtavannach – "The Monk's Isle" – in Loch Lomond. The heiress of the old Celtic line – "the Fair Maid of Luss" – had married Sir Robert Colquhoun of that Ilk in 1368, chief of a clan which came from Colquhoun near Dumbarton with lands along the Clyde around their ancient strong-hold of Dunglass. Colquhoun had fought for Robert the Bruce, and like others, was rewarded by title to lands – including a royal charter to all the ground within a "girth" of three miles about the Church of Luss to be a holy place of refuge. The Colquhouns took the surname of Luss from the name of their lands, and built their own stronghold at Rossdhu on a small promontary on the western shore of Loch Lomond.

However, although the place may once have been a religious sanctuary, the territory lay within that debatable land between the highlands and the lowlands, and the Colquhouns, a lowland clan by origin and inclination, had to be hard men to defend it. In 1439, the 10th Colquhoun, who was Sheriff of Dumbarton, was killed by a band of Western Islesmen led by MacLean of Duart while leading his followers in a last stand on the island of Inchmurrin in Loch Lomond. His grandson, Sir John of that Ilk, had his lands elevated into the "free Barony" of Luss by James II in 1457, with the right of "Pit and Gallows" – giving him local jurisdiction over life and death – in the exercise of which he and his successors displayed a considerable diligence, and the Gallowshill by Rossdhu marks the site of the Colquhoun "dule-tree" where their justice was summarily dispensed.

In 1592, Sir Humphrey Colquhoun, 16th of Luss, had been at feud with MacFarlane of Arrochar whose wife he had seduced. MacFarlane surprised him at this dalliance and pursued him past Rossdhu to his other castle of Bannachra. In the short siege, Colquhoun was shot in the back by his own brother (who was later hanged for the deed), and when the fight was over, MacFarlane had the body mutilated and the genitals served to his wife as a mocking dish for dinner. The MacFarlanes also kidnapped and ravished Colquhoun's daughter – "so little regard did those savage freebooters pay to the laws of chivalry that they brutally violated the person of Jean Colquhoun, the fair and helpless daughter of Sir Humphrey." These incidents served to demonstrate the savagery of life along the highland frontier, so that the events which now followed were arguably not so untypical. The Colquhouns were no strangers to cruelty. Nor were they the helpless victims of wild highlanders whose enmity they had earned.

Sir Humphrey Colquhoun was succeeded by his brother, Alexander 17th of Luss, who became a particular object of Argyll's ill-will. This Alexander Colquhoun was a friend of both MacAulay and the Duke of Lennox, and had signed a bond with Huntly in 1592, which made him seriously suspect in Argyll's eyes. His land marched with Argyll's own territory along the Lennox border – and the Campbell was an acquisitive neighbour. There were other political or family connections: Sir Humphrey's widow had married Campbell of Ardkinglas after the death of his wife, Annas Campbell of Glenorchy.

Most conveniently, the Colquhouns were also at serious feud with the Clan Gregor. During Sir Humphrey Colquhoun's time, two MacGregor packmen from Dunan in Rannoch had been to sell goods at the Glasgow Fair, and returning through Luss, had asked food and shelter from one of Colquhoun's tenants. To refuse such a request was almost unheard of in the highlands where there was a traditional rune of hospitality, and so when they were churlishly turned away, the two MacGregors decided to help themselves. Quartering at an empty shieling on the estate, they butchered a fat wedder out of the sheep-fold and next day continued on their way north. Unfortunately, through carelessness or stupidity they had chosen a most identifiable black sheep with a white tail. Its loss was quickly noticed, and the MacGregors were stopped and searched. When the distinctive fleece was found among their baggage they were promptly dragged to Rossdhu and hanged upon Colquhoun's gallows. This incident which caused the disastrous feud that followed gave rise to a highland proverb:

"Woe worth the day when the black wether with the white tail was ever lambed".

The wilder MacGregors therefore needed no urging to pillage the Colquhoun properties along the lowland border. Black John of the Mailcoat, Ian Dubh and Duncan, sons of Ewin the Tutor, James MacGregor son of Duncan of the Glen, and others of like spirit made numerous forays into the Lennox and committed "great riefs and herships" particularly upon Colquhoun of Luss.

Alasdair of Glenstrae subsequently swore that this was done at Argyll's instigation:

> He movit my brother and some of my friends to commit baith hership and slaughter upon the Laird of Luss. Also he persuadit myself, with messahe to weir against the Laird of Buchanan, whilk I did refuse; for the whilk I was continually boastit that he (Argyll) would be my unfriend; and when I did refuse his desire on that point, he enticit me with other messengers... to weir and trouble the Laird of Luss; whilk I behovit to do for his false boutgaits.[43]

Upon such persuasion, and possibly under pressure from his clansmen that he as chief should should lead them, on 4th June 1602, Glenstrae led some twenty MacGregors – his brother and his cousins supported by Neil Campbell the Traitor from Lochgoilhead, Duncan of the Glen and others of the gallows herd – into Luss and raided through Glenmulchan, reiving over 120 cattle. Colquhoun at once brought a claim against Argyll as being responsible under the Royal Commission for the behaviour of the Clan Gregor, but for some reason the Privy Council only called him to account under the General Band for his own identifiable Campbell clansmen. The Earl was ordered to produce Neil the Traitor and Duncan of the Glen, but the Council otherwise concluded that Colquhoun had failed to prove Argyll's responsibility for the rest. Argyll took no notice of the summons anyway.

The Clan Gregor's response was to do it again. Duncan MacEwin MacGregor led another raid into the Lennox and plundered Glenfinlas close to Rossdhu itself, lifting over 300 cows, 400 sheep and goats, and 100 horses (which were subsequently reset through the Campbell territories of Strachur, Appin, Lochgoilhead and Ardkinglas – thus suggesting Campbell connivance). However, this time there was some fighting, and the MacGregors killed a few of Colquhoun's people and wounded numbers more.

Colquhoun was determined upon retribution by some means, and consulted with his allies in Dumbarton – notably Semple of Fulwood who was Captain of the castle, and Thomas Fallasdale who was one of the more influential burgesses. Fallasdale hit upon a scheme to appeal to the King directly – and in such a way as would arouse his known antipathies towards bloodshed and disorder.

The court was then at Stirling, whither Colquhoun now rode, arriving on 21st December, and taking with him a number of women of his clan – purportedly the wives and mothers of those who had been cruelly killed or wounded by the MacGregors. Each woman carried a spear or pole with the "Bluidy sark" – the bloodstained shirt – of her man hanging from its point (and perhaps a few dipped in sheep's blood to make up the numbers) and paraded these gruesome relics before the horrified King. This public demonstration succeeded just as Colquhoun had hoped. James VI was suitably distressed, believing the women to be widows and orphans all, shockingly bereaved by an inhuman highland massacre, and there was no-one present who might have corrected such an impression. "The Clan Gregor", recorded the historian Sir Robert Gordon, "had none about the King to plead their cause, which proved hurtful to them". James VI, impassioned and confused, immediately granted a Commission of Fire and Sword to Colquhoun ordering him to proceed with all severity against the Gregarach.

That the Commission was possibly invalid – the legitimate authority still resting with Argyll – did not trouble Colquhoun, who now had the wooden cross of his clan dipped in goat's blood and sent by relays through the district to summon his people to their mustering place at the "Armoury Hillock" *(Cnoc Ealachainn)* near Rossdhu. He got reinforcement from the Buchanans (with whom he was now in amity, having married one of their laird's daughters) and the Royal Commission empowered him also to call out the fencible men of Dumbarton – armed with "hackbutts, jacks, spears, and steel bonnets" – raising in all some 300 horse and 500 foot .[44] With this considerable force he intended a military invasion of the inland glens.

Inevitably, word of these warlike preparations was carried to the MacGregors who had good warning of his coming. Submission was unthinkable, for no chief such as Alasdair would surrender his people, guilty or otherwise, to the vengeance of Colquhoun. But it was February and still hard winter. The scattered settlements of the Gregarach would be at their most vulnerable, the people dependent on their horded stores of winter provision – to abandon or lose the which would mean starvation for many, particularly the women and the bairns, and the older folk who could not survive on the high moors in such a climate, nor run with the broken men. Yet the MacGregors were insufficiently numerous to defend such a wide area in strength, so that they faced the prospect of being isolated and over-run.

The alternative was to mount a pre-emptive attack themselves, and so Alasdair sent out the gathering call of his clan – summoning his swordsmen from the Braes of Rannoch to join him at Balquhidder. They came under their local leaders – his brother Ian Dubh in his mail shirt, the three sons of Ewin the Tutor, MacGregor of Roro, and Robert Abrach, grandson of the fierce old Duncan Ladasach – some 400 men "boden in feir of weir, with halberts, poleaxes, twa-handed swords, bows and arrows, and other weapons". It was a small warband, outlandish compared with the enemy against whom they marched – some in pieces of ancient armour, most in *breacans* (the kilted plaid that hung in folds about the thigh), armed with old two handed claymores, lochaber axes, swords and targes, longbows, knives – each behind their chieftains and their pipers, eagle plume and sprigs of pine, battle banner and stirring pibroch – and in all the finest fighting men the clan could show.

They were joined by a few Campbells (possibly with the knowledge of Argyll), some Camerons, and a band of MacDonalds of Glencoe – wild caterans who came for the adventure and its hope of plunder.

The little army mustered in Balquhidder. According to local tradition the MacGregors marched over the hills to eastern Loch Lomondside, possibly by Glenarklet, and then took the ferry to reach the Pass of Arrochar and thence along the shores of Loch Long towards Garelochhead and the western end of Glenfruin. There, the track descended precipitously into the narrow glen, and Alasdair probably halted his men at Strone.

This circuitous route may have been intended to surprise Colquhoun, and one account suggests that he had already started north up Loch Lomond when news of Alasdair approaching from Loch Long caused him to make a forced march across the hills from Luss to Auchengaich in Glenfruin. There he found Alasdair and his clansmen holding the throat of the glen against him.

There is a tradition that Alasdair offered to parley – and promised to remove if Colquhoun would apologise, give blood payment to the MacGregor packmen's relatives, and himself disband his army. Such offer, if ever made, was intended to be rejected. Colquhoun had 300 horse and 500 foot and confident in these numbers and their lowland quality, he at once attacked – foolishly because his heavily armed horse who might have been effective on flatter, firmer ground could achieve no momentum in the rough wet land around the Auchengaich Burn.

Alasdair had picked his position to suit the fighting qualities of his clansmen, with the main body in the broken and boggy ground across the narrowest part of the glen, while a small force under his brother Ian Dubh nan Lurach, Black John of the Mail-coat, lay in ambush in a hollow close to Strone.

As the cavalry floundered in the difficult terrain, the MacGregors charged into Colquhoun's footsoldiers, coming immediately to close quarters and driving them down the glen to where Ian Dubh was waiting. But even as the trap sprang shut, Ian Dubh was killed by an arrow and thus was among the first to die.

Quickly didst thou turn, stripling MacLintock;
Thou hast slain Black John of the Mail-coat, great MacGregor's son.

The Gregarach got in among Colquhoun's cavalry, gaffing the riders out of their saddles with the great hooked Lochaber axes, hamstringing the horses, and destroying any vain attempt to rally. Quickly the fight turned into a rout, and the MacGregors in a pack chased the fleeing Colquhouns so that the killing continued to the gates of Rossdhu itself – Alexander Colquhoun with a horse killed under him barely escaping with his life.

At some stage and at some distance from this running fight a massacre occurred. It seems that some forty of Colquhoun's cavalry who had been unhorsed early in the battle, were stripped of their armour and herded together as prisoners under the watch of one Alan Oig MacIntnach of Glencoe. This wild MacDonald, excluded from the fighting but possibly becoming overheated by the scenes before him, stabbed them all to death, so that when Alasdair came back from the battle and inquired about his prisoners, the highlander would only brandish his bloody dagger and say "Ask that and God help me!"

Those killed in this incident accounted for nearly one third of the total casualties, since the Colquhouns were said to have lost 140 men. Alan Oig of Glencoe was later called to account for the crime, but in the meanwhile, rumours embellished the atrocity (the tradition given by Sir Walter Scott was that the prisoners were all schoolboys from Dumbarton come to watch the fight) and although Alan Oig was tried and convicted for it, other stories held that Alasdair and his Gregarach were resonsible.

Having decisively defeated Colquhoun, the MacGregors now harried the Lennox in real earnest, lifting 600 cattle, 800 sheep and goats, 240 horses and the entire removable wealth of Luss – much of which subsequently found its way into the possession of the Campbell tenants in Ardkinglas and Strachur. Throughout Colquhoun's lands they burned every house and barn.

Ian Dubh nan Lurach, their hero John of the Mail-coat, was buried where he fell, and a great stone placed above his grave to mark the spot. Among those who mourned him there were some perhaps who would later conclude that his death in battle was a luckier way to meet the end than the fate which was to be reserved for them.

CHAPTER 7

The Clan Proscribed

Luckless was thy foray, son of Red Gregor!
Thou wast my chiefest joy, thou has brought us sorrow enough tonight...
Deep was our grief, yestreen at the gloaming,
The chief of our clan, the first man of our race was the cause.
Dark was the glen, and long the farewell.

When news of the Field of Lennox, as the fight at Glenfruin was called, reached the Privy Council, they issued summonses against all who had taken part in the raid, calling the local landlords to take up arms against them and forbidding anyone to give them help or shelter. Then on 3rd April 1603, two days before travelling south to accept the throne of England, James VI, now out of all patience, gave the order to "extirpate Clan Gregor and to ruit oot their posteritie and name". An Act of the Privy Council proscribed the use of the names Gregor or MacGregor upon pain of death, and prohibited any who had borne those names from carrying weapons. Innocent persons were required to change their name by law, but all who had taken part in the slaughter at Glenfruin or gave food or shelter to Glenstrae's clansmen thereafter were denounced as rebels and outlaws and sentenced to death.

At the beginning, there was some indication that the original intention may not have been to prosecute the Act with the ruthlessness and vigour which its provisions portended. A letter from the Privy Council dated May 1603 informed the King in England that Alasdair (then in hiding) had accepted an offer that he and those of his people who had taken part in the raid should be banished, and that he had surrendered six young men of the clan (from the MacGregors of Roro) as hostages for surety that he would keep the bargain. The Privy Council requested the King to send a ship to Edinburgh to collect Alasdair and the other exiles, "seeing all these wha are to depart in whilk number the laird himself is ane, an to be in readiness here, ready to embark again Whitsuntide, being unable of themselves to defray their charges, furnish themselves of victual, or pay their fraught". But whether on account of expense or other malign influence, no ship ever came.

At first also, there were some who were willing to help the MacGregors as they had in the past. The cattle and livestock lifted after Glenfruin had been reset among the Campbell tenantry of Ardkinglas and Strachur. Some prominent lairds such as Campbell of Dragach and the Captain of Carrick gave them food and shelter for a while – until it became clear that the Privy Council intended this time to prosecute without favour, and possibly only the protection of Argyll himself saved them from punishment. Aulay MacAulay, who had sheltered Alasdair, was arrested and brought to trial, and escaped only through the influence of the Duke of Lennox who obtained a pardon from the King and gave him a place in his London household.

But for the MacGregors there was to be no reprieve as the Privy Council's policy hardened into one of total extermination. Warrants to kill MacGregors were put on public sale as if they were licensed game to be killed for sport. A bounty was offered for the head of any MacGregor with an additional reward of all the dead man's possessions – and if the killer was himself an outlaw, he would be pardoned for his past offences.

Such inducements gave new effect to the Commissions of Fire and Sword – and there was no shortage of bounty hunters ready to claim the rewards. Archibald Dalzell, a younger son of Dalzell of that Ilk, who had been outlawed for crimes of violence and rape, killed two MacGregors and was one of the first to claim his blood-money and his pardon. Colquhoun of Camstrodden won a similar pardon by capturing two MacGregors and delivering them to prison in Edinburgh – but one of them "barbarously stickit himself"(committed suicide) while awaiting execution, and so cheated the mob of some promised entertainment.

Such men were abetted by the Gregarach's long-time enemies who chiefly led the process and whose zeal for the cause led them to exceed all previous efforts to cleanse the inland glens – most notably the Colquhouns, venomous in revenge; Black Duncan of Glenorchy who trained a pack of blood-hounds to track down the fugitives; and Stewart of Ardvorlich, who, remembering Drummond-Ernoch, implacably put to death every MacGregor whom he could lay hold on – men, women, young and old. All worked with the sanction of a Privy Council which incited them to treat the MacGregors as vermin, barbarous, Godless malefactors and wolves, and "to slaughter and mutilate them and to raise fire".

Inexorably, this grim hunting produced its human trophies – and those still alive were sent to Edinburgh for public execution. On 18th April 1603 four MacGregors were hanged at Boroughmuir; on 20th May three more on the Castlehill; on 5th July two more; in August more. There was Gregor

Gair, too old to fight but whose three sons had joined the foray, arrested
and hanged for resetting Alasdair after he came from Glenfruin "with the
bloody hand".[45] Other crimes were added to the account – Duncan
McAllaster Vrek who had stripped the Laird of Struan's mansion of all its
furnishings worth £1,000; Donald MacClerich who had been one of a
band of reivers who stole nine cows in Atholl two years previously; John
Ammonoche MacGregor who had stolen six sheep eight years before; and
Malcolm MacCoull Clerich who had not only sheltered Alasdair after
Glenfruin but had allegedly been in the vicinity when a servant of my Lord
Atholl was killed over thirty years bygone: each remembered and brought
to book. In all, and aside from the heads taken by the bounty killers and
delivered to the Privy Council, some fifty MacGregors were publicly
hanged in Edinburgh during the eight months following Glenfruin.

The Gregarach did not tamely submit. Stories abound of remarkable
escapes and vicious skirmishes in the inland glens, for the outlaws when
cornered sold their lives dearly, and often the hunted turned and ran down
the hunters. There is the tale of a MacGregor pursued by Black Duncan's
pack of bloodhounds who hid behind a waterfall in Glenfalloch and shot
the leading dog through the wall of spray before getting safe away to fight
and run again. Another relates how a friendly highlander in Glenlyon
helped a fleeing MacGregor to escape by killing the dog that was tracking
him with a shrewdly aimed kick to the head – and then told the pursuing
Campbells with a sly honesty that he "had not laid a hand on it". There is
a story that Alasdair of Glenstrae himself with a small band of followers
came upon a bounty killer with three MacGregor heads in a sack, and
promptly hanged him from the nearest tree.[46]

But although the MacGregor clansmen, enured to hardship, could live
off the country, fight and escape from their pursuers and survive on the
high moors, the relentless persecution took a terrible toll on the women
and children, the old and the helpless. With winter approaching, Alasdair's
people were destitute. This year there would be no harvest; no Gregarach
cattle driven to the fair at Crieff; no salted meat for winter provision; no
cows to keep for lifting into the pastures in the spring. Their settlements
were burned out; what little they had was pillaged or destroyed. Their
position became steadily more desperate.

It was in this situation that on 2nd October 1603, Alasdair received a
message from Campbell of Ardkinglas inviting him to his house at the head
of Loch Fyne. He went, unsuspecting and probably alone. Over the years
and during his dealings with Argyll, Alasdair had kept faith with
Ardkinglas with whom he recognised the highland bond of kinship, and

he may therefore have trusted Ardkinglas as having some reciprocal feeling or sense of honour – "the man I did maist trust unto".

But Ardkinglas, weak as he had always proved himself to be, with the Cawdor conspiracy upon his conscience and dependent upon Argyll whom he was desperate to please – and now married withal to a Colquhoun widow – had planned to play the role of Judas. When Alasdair arrived he was immediately taken by a band of armed Campbells who were lying in wait.

Ardkinglas's house stood on a small peninsula formed by the waters of the Kinlas and Loch Fyne. From there the overland route to Argyll's castle at Inveraray crossed the head of Glenfyne and followed the loch shore to Glenshira – some eleven miles on foot and potentially dangerous should the Gregarach have had news of the chief's capture and planned to attempt a rescue along the way. Ardkinglas therefore had Alasdair bound and put in a boat with five armed guards to be transported across the loch and so delivered to the MacCailein Mor.

However, Alasdair contrived a daring escape. In his later confession he would state simply that "God did relieve me unto liberty, maist narrowly", but tradition has it that he worked loose from his bonds and pushing the nearest guard overboard, dived into the loch and swam for the shore, to reach eventually the shelter of the woods.

The hunting of the MacGregors continued. That autumn before the snow and rain made the ground impassable, Robert Campbell, one of Black Duncan's younger sons, led a large force of Campbells in pursuit of the Gregarach, and this time their once inviolable sanctuary at Rannoch was no refuge. There was some fierce fighting in which "seven Campbell gentlemen" were killed but the MacGregors also took heavy losses and were progressively driven out of that heartland which had been theirs by sword right and immemorial possession.

Wet autumn gave place to freezing winter and for the outlaws the situation grew steadily worse, when, during the latter days of December 1603, discreet messages from the Earl of Argyll found their way by some means to where Alasdair was hiding. These dissociated the MacCailein Mor from the attempted betrayal by his clansman Ardkinglas, and Argyll offered to broke himself for Alasdair's pardon if he would give himself up on suitable terms. (In fact Argyll was simultaneously writing to the Privy Council claiming that he was putting himself to great toil and expense to reach some settlement.) Argyll further offered to provide safe escort across the border into England so that once again Alasdair might have an opportunity to seek his own pardon directly from the King.

For Alasdair in his situation, the proposal perhaps contained the element of a desperate logic. He had successfully appealed to the King's mercy once before and the outcome had been favourable. He was still the King's household man. Aulay MacAulay in the train of the Duke of Lennox was a friend at court. Argyll knew if anyone did, the true story behind Glenfruin – and was his only protection however covert or ambivalent against his greatest enemy, Black Duncan of Glenorchy. Upon these or other considerations Alasdair agreed to a secret personal meeting with Argyll in the presence of a "mutual friend" at which, he afterwards claimed, the Campbell gave him a written undertaking that he would guarantee his safe conduct into England. At the end of this meeting, Argyll cunningly let Alasdair go.

On a midwinter's evening somewhere among the inland glens, Alasdair of Glenstrae took farewell of his clan. Then, on 4th January 1604, together with Ian Dubh MacEwin and three others of his clansmen, he surrendered himself to the MacCailein Mor. Argyll accompanied them to Edinburgh and ten days later they were escorted to Berwick and the Border. In keeping with "ane hielandman's promise" they were allowed to cross into England where they were immediately rearrested by the Edinburgh town Guard and taken captive back to the Scottish capital. (No details are known of the actual incident, other than the fact that the "broun naig" which Alasdair was riding was somehow killed in the affair, since one John Murray who had presumably provided the horse, claimed twenty crowns in compensation.)

They reached Edinburgh on the evening of 18th January, and Alasdair with the other MacGregors would be formally arraigned upon the following day. Scottish legal practice provides for a preliminary statement to be taken from prisoners before trial, and on the night of 18th January Alasdair was visited by Mr James Primrose, Clerk of the Council together with the lawyers assigned to conduct the prosecution. Alasdair freely consented to make a statement, and since he was illiterate this was probably given largely at his dictation. They headed it "Confession of Alasdair MacGregor of Glenstrae", and it convicted him out of his own mouth – as no doubt was the intention. But in a truer perspective, it stands also as his Accusation against Argyll, for it is a simple man's account of the events preceding and after the slaughter at Glenfruin – in which the whole sordid story, his confusion, despair, and ultimate betrayal is ingenuously revealed. Fragments of this statement have been quoted earlier, but as evidence it deserves to be presented in its entirety. Alasdair must have known that he was doomed, and had no longer cause to lie – if he had ever done so. It is his last testament. Indeed, it is all that is left of him.

I, Alasdair MacGregor of Glenstrae, confess here before God that I have been persuadit, movit, and enticit, as I am now presently accusit and troublit for; als, gif I had usit counsel or command of the man that has enticit me, I wad have done and committit sindry high murders mair. For truly, sin I was first his Majesty;'s man, I never could be at ane ease, by my Lord of Argyll's falseheid and inventions; for he causit MacLean and Glen Chamroun *(Clan Cameron)* to commit hership and slaughter in my rowme of Rannoch, the whilk causit my puir men thereafter to beg and steal. Alsua, thereafter, he movit my brother and some of my friends to commit baith hership and slaughter upon the laird of Luss.

Alsua, he persuadit myself, with message, to weir agains the laird of Buchanan, whilk I did refuse; for the whilk I was continually boastit that he would be my unfriend: and when I did refuse his desire in that point, then he enticit me with other messengers, as by the laird of MacNachtan and others of my friends, to weir and trouble the laird of Luss: which I behovit to do for his false boutgaits.

Then, when he saw I was at ane strait, he causit me to trow he was my guid friend: but I did perceive he was slow therein. Then I made moyan to please his Majesty and Lords of Council, baith of service and obedience, to punish faltours and to safe innocent men; and when Argyll was made foreseen thereof, he enticit me to stay and start fra thae conditions, causing me to understand that I was deceivit; but with fair words, to put me in ane snare, that he might get the lands of Kintyre in feyell fra his Majesty, began to put at me and my kin.

The whilk Argyll inventit, maist shamefully, and persuadit the laird of Ardkinglas to deceive me, wha was the man I did maist trust into; but God did relieve me in the meantime unto liberty, maist narrowly. Nevertheless Argyll made the open bruit that Ardkinglas did all that falseheid without his knowledge. Whilk he did entice me, with oft and sindry messages, that he was mak my peace and safe my life and lands, only to punish certain faltours of my kin, and my innocent freinds to renounce their surname and live peacably. Upon the whilk conditions, he was sworn by an aith to his friends, and they sworn to me; and als, I have his warrant and handwrit thereupon: the whilk promise, gif they be honestly keepit, I let God be judge! And at our meeting, in our awn chalmer, he was sworn to me, in witness of his awn friend.

Attour I confess, before God, that he did all his crafty diligence
to entice me to slay and destroy the laird Ardincaple, MacAulay, for
ony gains, kindness or friendship he might do or give me. The whilk
I did refure, in respect of my faithful promise made to MacAulay of-
before. Alsua, he did all the diligence he could, to move me to slay
the laird of Ardkinglas in like manner: bot I never grantit thereto;
through the whilk he did envy me grettumly.

And now, seeing God and man sees it is greediness of warldly gear
causes him to put at me and my kin, and not the weal of the realm,
nor to pacify the samyn, nor to his Majesty's honour, bot to put down
innocent men, to cause their puir bairns and infants beg, and puir
women to perish for hunger, when they are harried of their gear; the
whilk, I pray God that these faults light not upon his Majesty here-
after, nor upon his succession. Wherefore, I had beseek God, that
his Majesty knew the verity, that at this hour I wad be content to tak
banishment, with all my kin that was at the laird of Luss's slaughter,
and all others of them that ony fault can be laid to their charge; and
his Majesty of his mercy, to let puir innocent men and young bairns
pass to liberty, and learn to live as innocent men.

The whilk I wad fulfil, bot ony kind of fail; whilk wad be mair to
the will of God and his Majesty'd honour, nor the greedy cruel form
that is devisit, only for love of gear, having neither respect to God
nor honesty.[47]

The following day – 19th October 1603 – Alasdair and his four clansmen
were tried before a jury of their enemies, who included Thomas Fallasdale
burgess of Dumbarton whose kinsmen Thomas and James Fallasdale had
been killed at Glenfruin; the Captain of Dumbarton, another of
Colquhoun's creatures; Colin Campbell of Glenorchy, Black Duncan's
eldest son; and Menzies of that Ilk who was now able to regain his 32 merkland at Rannoch which the MacGregors had held by sword-right.

The verdict was "guilty of Treason" and the Doomster pronounced the
sentence:

That the saids persons be tane to the Mercat-Cross of Edinburgh,
and there to be hangit on ane gibbet while they be deid; and thereafter their heids, legs, arms, and remanent parts of their bodies to be
quarterit and put upon public places, and their hale lands, heritages,
annual rents, taks, steadings, rowmes, possessions, corns, cattle,
guids, gear, and sums of money pertaining to them, to be forfaultit,

escheat, and inbrought to our sovereign lord's use, as convict of the said treasonable crimes.

Their execution was carried out the following day, and since four clansmen were considered insufficient spectacle to grace the calvary of so notorious a chief, the six MacGregors of Roro surrendered as hostages the previous May were hanged beside them – although these had not been tried or convicted of any crime and "were young men and reputed honest for their own parts". Alasdair as chief "wes hangit his awin hicht above the rest of his friendis". When the body was cut down, his head was sent to Dumbarton and fixed on a spike above the town tolbooth.

Argyll never deigned to answer the charges implicit in Glenstrae's Confession, and three years later for his loyal services against the Clan Gregor he duly obtained the reward which he had coveted when a grateful King granted him "in feyell" the lands of Kintyre.

*   *   *

The Clan Gregor spontaneously rose to avenge their chief, and raided into the territories of Campbell of Glenorchy with terrible ferocity. Even Black Duncan is said to have cowered before this eruption of their anger as they cut a great swathe of devastation through Culdares and Duneaves in Fortingall, Crannuich in Breadalbane, Glenfalloch, Bochastel, and burned his newly built castle at Achallader – doing him grief as he claimed to the amount of over £66,666 Scots. But the MacGregors could not keep the field in strength, being obliged also to defend their settlements, and operated thereafter in smaller bands.

The Privy Council meanwhile proceeded with its policy to accomplish "the extermination of that wicked, unhappie and infamous race of lawles lymmaris, callit MacGregour" until they were "alluterlie extirpat and rooted out". Nobody who had previously borne the name MacGregor could assemble in a group exceeding four persons. A free pardon was offered to anyone who surrendered to the authorities and brought with him the head of another MacGregor of equal rank – while two or three heads of common clansmen could also purchase immunity. The MacGregor womenfolk, however, were not to be hanged, but branded on the face with a red-hot key before being transported to a lowland reservation. But they too might escape the branding iron if they would betray a husband or a brother. Children were also sent to lowland reservations, but many were taken by the lairds engaged in the pursuit who turned them to profit by demanding exorbitant expenses from the government to cover the costs of their upkeep. These and other provisions were embodied in an Act of Parliament of 1607 which added the prohibition that children might not take the names of their former parents lest a fresh generation of the accursed clan might emerge and cause more trouble in the future. (A further Statute of 1633 ruled that no clergyman was to baptise any male child of the MacGregors.)

Thus the persecution of the MacGregors went on, with the bounty killers enjoying open season in hunting down the outlawed Gregarach, who were homeless, friendless, and with the death of their chief, now leaderless and in all respects a "broken clan".

Many stories and traditions still remember the escapes, the savage encounters and the atrocities of this time.

Some MacGregors got away. At Invervar there was a "sheltering bed" – a hollow in an overhanging rock, fourteen foot long, six feet broad and four feet high, with a spring of clear water at one end, where Iain Buidhe Ruadh MacGregor (John of the Yellow-reddish Hair) went into hiding. One day, Campbell of Lawers who was one of the most ruthless of the hunters, waylaid his wife as she went to obtain food, and terrified of the branding, she agreed to reveal the hiding place by walking to and fro in front of the rock at dawn the following day. Lawers' men rushed the place, but the MacGregor, suspicious perhaps of his wife's behaviour that morning, heard a noise and disappeared into the mountains.

Others were less fortunate. At Rannoch a number of MacGregors hid in a rocky outcrop on the shoulder of Schiehallion overlooking the Tummel in what became known as "MacGregor's Cave", but they were discovered and flushed out by a force of Glenorchy's men and driven down the hillside to the bank of the Tummel. Two were shot as they tried to cross the river, and the rest were put to death along the shore.

A number of MacGregors took refuge in another cave a mile north-west of the Falls of Tummel at the east end of the loch. It was located at the top of a rocky precipice, accessible only by a steep and narrow pathway so that only one person could approach at a time. But it proved a trap with no alternative exit to escape, and when they were surprised and overrun by an overwhelming force of Campbells some of the Gregarach climbed into a tree which grew out over the precipice and tried to hang from its branches. The Campbells hacked their arms off so that they fell to their deaths on the rocks below.

Robert Campbell, Black Duncan of Glenorchy's younger son, led out another strong force to avenge the burning of his father's lands, and drove a band of MacGregors onto the lower slopes of Meall Buidh north of Glenlyon. The Gregarach turned at bay and some of their best swordsmen fell in the desperate fighting which followed. Many were also captured and taken back for execution. Eighteen were hanged in Edinburgh for the raid into Glenfalloch in addition to "sundry others hangit there and in other places whose names were superfluous to write". Black Duncan got some satisfaction.

From 1610–1613 the Earl of Argyll took the leading part in the extermination of the Gregarach and prosecuted the business with ruthless efficiency. In 1611 the Privy Council was still paying bounty money for the heads of MacGregors delivered to Edinburgh. In 1613 Campbell of Lawers was claiming expenses for the upkeep of seventy MacGregor boys under fourteen whose fathers had been killed and was disputing other rewards and costs with Black Duncan of Glenorchy. Argyll himself turned such a profit from the fines and bounties that the envious King in England demanded a share of twenty two and a half per cent.

By 1613, the cleansing was virtually complete. Probably few more than a score or so MacGregors still held out in the mountains. Of Alasdair of Glenstrae's immediate family, twenty two had been hanged, four beheaded, five killed in battle, and four shot in the back.

Most of the survivors found shelter among their neighbours whose names they took (Murray, Drummond, Miller – ironically the most common one was Campbell), living peacably "as innocent men", but keeping in their hearts the ancient pride of their race – "E'en do and spare nocht" – and waiting for a day when they might claim their true name again.

A number of die-hards, whether in small bands or alone, skulked as outlaws in the hills, finding refuge in the dark quarries and the remoter straths among the inland glens. The haunting Lament of MacGregor of Roro evokes the lonely, unquiet existence of the highland fugitive:

Now a rede I would rede thee, and thereupon think well thou:
When thou goest to the hostel, but a single cup drink thou.
Stand and drink. Be thou ware of men that look on:
Be the cup deep or shallow, drinkit down, and be gone.

Make winter thy autumn, the wolf-days thy summer:
Thy bed be the bare rock, and light be thy slumber.
For though scarce be the squirrel, there's a way got to find her,
And though proud be the falcon, there are deft hands can bind her.

CHAPTER 8

Bringing the Highlands and Islands to Obedience

You stole green pleasant Islay from us by trickery,
and Kintyre with its fertile plains.

Although the fate of the MacGregors was the extreme case, they were not the only example of a clan dispossessed of its ancestral lands under a lowland policy of highland cleansing. In 1529, James V had signed an order to the Earl of Moray and others to put down disorders among the Clan Chattan and "leave no creature living of that clan, except priests, women and bairns"(who were to be deported to Shetland). Lowland attitudes towards the Gaelic people grew steadily more hostile during the latter part of the 16th century, and James VI would display a prejudice that became racist in its expression, haranguing Parliament on the inferiority of the Hebrideans and sententiously advising his son (later Charles I): "As for the Highlands, I shortly comprehend them all in two sorts of people: the one that dwelleth in our mainland that are barbarous and yet mixed with some show of civility; the other that dwelleth in the Isles and are all utterly barbarous".

The subduing of the Highlands and "The Danting of the Isles" became an abiding preoccupation of the government in Scotland, but lacking the resources itself, the Crown devolved responsibility for enforcing law and order to those powerful nobles whose loyalty to the sovereign was congenially compatible with the task of putting down unruly neighbours and extending their own territories into the lands of their hereditary enemies. The most pre-eminent beneficiaries of this policy were Argyll (Campbells), Huntly (Gordons) and Seaforth (Mackenzies) who were at the same time both feudal superiors of large tracts of land and also chiefs of powerful clans in their own right. Although sometimes at rivalry with each other, their methods were largely the same.

*   *   *

The Gordons in Aberdeenshire were of feudal rather than Gaelic origin – probably descended from a Norman family who had crossed to England with the Conqueror and later settled in Scotland at the invitation of David I. Like the Campbells, they owed their rise to the gratitude of Robert the Bruce who granted Strathbogie in Aberdeenshire, forfeited by the pro-Balliol Earl of Atholl, to Sir Adam Gordon of Berwickshire. Through marriage with a Keith who was the heiress of a Fraser mother, they acquired Aboyne, Glentanar, and Glenmuick. When the male line died out the Gordon heiress married a Seton whose son, created Earl of Huntly in 1445, revived the name and arms of Gordon. In 1451 he became Lord of Badenoch and during the next generation the family acquired further lands in Aberdeenshire and Banffshire. Like the Earls of Argyll, this power qualified them for lowland appointments and the Earls of Huntly came traditionally to hold the commission of Lieutenant of the North.

Firmly established in Aberdeenshire, the second and third Earls of Huntly (George, died 1501: Alexander, died 1524) fixed their ambitions on the lands to the North. Their tactic was to secure the marriage of a younger son to the daughter of the family to be despoiled, and then obtain a "brieve of idiocy" against the heir, declare the second son to be a bastard, murder any other sons who would dispute the matter and claim the lands and title through the heiress. By such means the Gordons acquired the Earldom of Sutherland during the early years of the 16th century.

In 1560 the 4th Earl of Huntly tried to acquire the lands of Ogilvie of Findlater by similarly devious means. The English ambassador in Scotland reported to Elizabeth I's Secretary William Cecil that Huntly had convinced Ogilvie of Findlater that his own son and heir was planning to deprive him of his reason by locking him up and denying him any sleep as a basis for obtaining a brieve of idiocy. "This being revealed and sure tokens given unto his father that this was true, he thought just cause be given unto him why his son should not succeed, and having no other issue, by the persuasion of his wife (who was a Gordon) gave the whole land unto John Gordon who after the death of the said Findlater married her and so had right to the whole living. To see how God hath plagued the iniquity of the same woman, which in one month after her marriage John Gordon casteth his fancy with another and locked her up in a close chamber where yet she remaineth".

Possession of Sutherland stimulated the Gordons' ambition to acquire the region of Strathnaver which was occupied under immemorial title by the Clan MacKay. Just as Argyll had seen the MacGregors as a potential instrument to pursue his policy against the Colquhouns, so also the Earls of Huntly hoped that feudal superiority over Strathnaver would place at their disposal a vassal army of MacKays whom they intended to launch against the Sinclair Earls of Caithness as their next target in the process of northward expansion.

In fact, MacKay's title was good, having been confirmed by the Lord of the Isles in 1506 and by James V under the Great Seal in 1539. But the Gordons' acquisitiveness was extremely persistent. The MacKay heir was captured by the English at the battle of Solway Moss in 1542, and in the dynastic squabble which followed the King's death, the MacKays for reasons of their own followed the Duke of Lennox who was espoused to the causes of reform and the English interest. The pro-English faction was prejudiced by the savagery displayed by Henry VIII and support in Scotland swung behind the French Queen Mother, Mary of Lorraine. The Earl of Huntly quickly transferred his allegiance to her when it became clear that her pro-French policies were gaining the ascendancy, and was duly rewarded with the Earldom of Moray. MacKay, who was also first cousin of the true, dispossessed heir to the Sutherland Earldom, unwisely invaded Sutherland and this gave Huntly the excuse to raid into Strathnaver. The Gordons "invaded and spoiled, carrying from thence a great booty of goods and cattle in the year of God 1551". However, Mary of Lorraine, and for a period, Mary Queen of Scots refused to oblige Huntly by granting him feudal superiority over Strathnaver. In fact, during the early years of Mary's reign the Gordons suffered a temporary setback when the young Queen sided with the protestant Lords of the Congregation and took back the Earldom of Moray which she gave to her illegitimate half-brother, James Stewart (later Regent). Huntly, who was leader of the catholic faction, resorted to rebellion but was defeated and killed at the Battle of Corrichie. His two sons were also captured after the battle and convicted of treason. The heir, George, 5th Earl, was later restored but the younger, John (he who had acquired the lady and lands of Findlater) was executed at Aberdeen. Their entire estates were forfeited as too were those of the Earldom of Sutherland.

But gradually, as the political situation worsened, an unsuccessful revolt by Moray persuaded Mary of a need to rehabilitate the Gordons as potential supporters, and they crept back to power beneath the Queen's skirts. The new Earl of Huntly was restored to all his father's properties (but not the Earldom of Moray) and appointed Chancellor. The Gordon Earl of Sutherland also recovered his land and possessions under the Great Seal. Just before Moray compelled her to abdicate, Huntly used his power to extract from the embattled Queen the prize which he had coveted for so long – namely that MacKay should be dispossessed of Strathnaver on grounds of bastardy. The last Parliament of her reign recorded that Mary "granted and gave heritably to her trusty cousin and Councillor George, Earl of Huntly, Lord Gordon and Badenoch, her Highness' Chancellor, all and sundry the lands and baronies... which pertained heritably of before to umquile Donald MacKay of Farr... and pertaining to our Sovereign... by reason the said umquile Donald was born and deceased bastard without lawful heir of his body gotten or lawful disposition made by him of his lands and goods during his lifetime." (In fact Donald MacKay's legitimacy had been formally confirmed under the Privy Seal in 1511.) Upon the excuse of bringing all Scotland to "universal obedience" it was a cynical example of how a powerful noble could manipulate lowland law to legalise the dispossession of a highland clan.

The chief, Aodh MacKay, according to the Gordon historian, was forced to submit to both the Earls of Huntly and Sutherland, "and upon his faithful promise to assist Earl Alexander (Sutherland) against the Earl of Caithness in time coming, obtained from the Earl of Huntly the heritable gift and title of the lands of Strathnaver for the sum of £3000 scots. Yet Huntly still retained the superiority of Strathnaver to himself." In 1588 Aodh's heir, Uisdean MacKay submitted entirely to the Earl of Sutherland, probably because this suited Gordon policy in pursuing their quarrel with the Sinclair Earl of Caithness.

In 1567, John Earl of Sutherland had been poisoned by a member of his own family leaving a fifteeen year old heir, Alexander. The Sinclair Earl of Caithness used his influence as Justiciar of the North to be appointed the boy's Guardian, and then took further advantage of his position to marry him to one of his daughters (a lady of twice his age). The Gordons retaliated by raiding Dunrobin and abducting the Sutherland heir. A divorce from his Sinclair wife was obtained upon the claim of her adultery with MacKay. The Sutherland heir was then married to a Gordon of Huntly who had previously been the wife of the Earl of Bothwell before he shuffled her off to marry the Queen.

The MacKays, however, did not prove a pliant tool against the Earl of Caithness as the Gordons had intended since they were closely connected to the Sinclairs by marriage through successive generations. After Aodh MacKay died in 1572 and his son Uisdean became Alexander of Sutherland's vassal, he was also forced to divorce his Sinclair wife in favour of a Gordon, but since this made Uisdean MacKay Alexander of Sutherland's uncle, just in case their own male line should fail, the Gordons persuaded James VI to grant them a charter barring this Gaelic branch of the family from any future succession to the title or lands of Gordon. (The son of Uisdean MacKay and Jean Gordon subsequently became Lord Reay.) Such was the Gordons' ambivalent attitude to matrimonial convention.　　　　　　　　　　　　　　　　　　　　　•

A document written by Sir Robert Gordon, tutor to Alexander of Sutherland during his minority, reveals the cultural prejudice against the highlanders. Advising the young man on how to treat his uncle MacKay, the Tutor tells him:

Use MacKay rather as your vassal than as your companion, and because they are usually proud and arrogant, let them know that you are their superior. If you shall happen to buy or purchase any lands in Strathnaver, use kindly the natives you find upon the land, that thereby you may purchase their love and alienate their minds from MacKay. Be not too hard-handed to them at first, for by a little freeness and liberality you may gain them, which is the nature of all highlanders... Yet by progress of time I wish you to send some of your own people at dwell among them. Use your diligence to take away the relics of the Irish barbarity which as yet remains in your country, to wit, the Irish language and the habit. Purge your country piece by piece from that uncivil kind of clothes, such as plaids, mantles, trews, and blue bonnets. Make severe acts against those that shall wear them. Cause the inhabitants of the country to clothe themselves as the most civil provinces of the Kingdom do, with doublet, hose, cloaks, and hats, which they may do with less charges than the other. It is no excuse which some would pretend, alleging that uncivil habit to be lightest in the mountains... The Irish language cannot so soon be extinguished. To help this, plant schools in every corner of the country to instruct the youth to speak English.

In the Highland Region, Huntly's feudal claims brought him into conflict with the Clan Chattan of Badenoch, and the intervention of the Bonnie Earl of Moray had been one of the points of contention that led to his assassination (Chapter 4).

George, 6th Earl of Huntly went briefly into exile after the Battle of Glenlivat, but was subsequently pardoned and created a Marquis in 1599, when he took up the feud against the Clan MacKintosh with renewed vigour. Sir Walter Scott, in "Tales of a Grandfather" recounts two stories which illustrate the savagery with which such quarrels were pursued.

William MacIntosh surprised and burned the Gordon castle at

Auchindoun, and Huntly swore to take revenge. The Gordons and their allies invaded Badenoch, and MacIntosh, seeing his clan threatened with extermination, decided to surrender himself to Huntly and atone for the offence. However, he chose a time when the Marquis of Huntly was absent, in the notion that his wife would be less implacable and more ready to reach some accomodation. Accordingly, he presented himself at Huntly's castle at the Bog of Gight to plead his cause and ask mercy for his clan. He was received in the castle kitchen by the Marchioness who took a severe view of the matter and told him that Huntly was so deeply offended that he had sworn to have MacIntosh's head on a block. MacIntosh said that he would accept any condition if it meant the saving of his clan, and intending it as a gesture, undid the collar of his doublet and bared his neck. Whereupon, at a sign from the lady, the cook promptly beheaded him with a kitchen cleaver.

The second tradition relates to a feud between Huntly and the Farquharsons of Deeside after the latter had killed a gentleman called Gordon of Brackley. Huntly was accompanied by the Laird of Grant who was related to Brackley, and their two forces went along Deeside from each end, the Grants from the head of the valley and the Gordons moving upstream killing all the Farquharsons between them. Most of the Farquharson men and women were butchered without mercy, but when the massacre was over, Huntly rounded up some 200 orphans whose parents had been killed and took them back to the Bog of Gight.

About a year later, the Laird of Grant chanced to be dining at Huntly's castle. After the meal, the Marquis offered to show him "some rare sport" and took him to a balcony overlooking the main kitchen where Grant saw that the food scraps had been tipped into a large pig trough. At a sign from Huntly a hatch "like that of a dog kennel" was raised, but there rushed into the kitchen not a pack of hounds as Grant expected, but a mob of wild children who fought over the food like animals. Asked by the horrified Grant who these unfortunate creatures were to be fed like swine, Huntly aswered that they were the children of the Farquharsons whom they had killed the previous summer. Grant secured their release (Huntly having become bored with the joke) and took the children back to Castle Grant where they were dispersed among his own people and took the name of Grant – although tradition avers that their descendants continued to be called The Race of the Trough "to distinguish them from the families of the tribe into which they were adopted."

The severity with which Huntly indulged his prejudice against the Gaelic clans may have been one of the qualities which prompted James VI to prefer him for commissions of genocide in furtherance of a policy to cleanse and recolonise the Western Isles.

In 1598 a grossly distorted report on the resources of the Hebridean Islands greatly exaggerated their value as a potential source of revenue for the Crown, and in particular described the Isle of Lewis as "the most fertile and commodious part of the whole realm... enriched with an incredible fertility of corn, store of fishing and other necessaries surpassing far the plenty of any part of the inland." When therefore, the MacLeods of Dunvegan and Lewis did not produce their title deeds as required by the Act of 1597 (Chapter 1) the lands of Dunvegan, Harris, Glenelg and the Island of Lewis were declared to be at the King's disposal, who leased them to a company of lowland colonists led by the Duke of Lennox known as The Fife Adventurers. In establishing their settlements they were to employ "slaughter, mutilation, fire raising and other inconveniences" to expel the native population. An Act of Parliament justified the "rooting out of the barbarous inhabitants" on the grounds that they were "void of any knowledge of God or His Religion" and had "given themselves over to all kinds of barbarity and inhumanity".

However, the hired troops whom the Adventurers sent to seize Lewis were driven off by the islanders, and in 1602, the King granted a fresh Lieutenancy to Lennox and a second to Huntly. Mackenzie of Kintail also came forward with support for the project and was rewarded with membership of the Privy Council. In fact Mackenzie's intention at this stage was secretly to undermine the Fife Adventurers since he himself had an interest in the Barony of Lewis.

The Mackenzies had been one of the few northern clans not displaced by the Lords of the Isles when they acquired the Earldom of Ross, and after the forfeiture of the Lordship they expanded along the western seaboard from Kintail ("Head of Salt Water") and their heartlands of Glenshiel, Glenlichd and Glenelchaid to Eddrachillis, taking possession of the territories which had been held by the MacDonalds of Glengarry and the MacLeods of Lewis. By marriage and purchase they acquired the estates around Loch Broom, the church lands of Applecross, and by 1603 had pushed the MacDonalds out of Loch Alsh and Loch Carron, and displaced the MacLeods from Gairloch. Eastwards their power base rested on the rich lands around the Cromarty Firth and the Black Isle (where they acquired extensive church property after the Reformation) and their Royal Charters to Strathconan, Strathgarve and Strathbran. Ambitious and land hungry, in the North the Mackenzies had become a major force in the highlands second only to the Campbells and the Gordons.

Mackenzie's interest in Lewis stemmed from the fact that the MacLeods of Lewis – the *Siol Torquill* – who in addition held also the lands of Trotternish in Skye, Raasay, Coigeach in Wester Ross and Assynt in Sutherland, were split by a familiy quarrel from which he stood to profit. The MacLeod chief, Ruari, had divorced his first wife who was a Mackenzie of Kintail and denied the paternity of her son Torquil Connanach in favour of Torquil Dubh, his son by a second marriage. But the government had recognised the claim of Torquil Connanach and he, being himself without male heirs, had handed over the MacLeod charters to the head of his mother's family – Mackenzie of Kintail – conveying to him the Barony of Lewis. But the people had supported Torquil Dubh so that to date, Mackenzie had only obtained de facto occupation of Torquil Connanach's mainland estates.

Shortly after James VI departed for London, a second invasion of Lewis also failed and the King commissioned Huntly to equip a further expedition at his own expense in return for the reward of "the whole of the North Isles except Skye and Lewis in feu". Huntly accepted, confirming that "his Lordship offers to take in hand the service of settling the North Isles… and to put an end to that service by extirpation of the barbarous people of the Isles within a year."

The Privy Council protested: "Anent the Lieutenancy, they think it likewise unreasonable that the King's power should be put in the hends of a subject to conquer lands to himself" – which was a somewhat hypocritical complaint since this was how such commissions had regularly been used, and the more likely reason was their objection to further power being put in the hands of a catholic noble. The King wrote again to Huntly in 1607 reminding him that his orders were "the extirpating of the barbarous people in those bounds" and insisting that the islands were to be colonised by civilised people who did not speak Gaelic. In the event Huntly did not accomplish this atrocity since he fell out with the King over the feu duties that he would be required to pay. Meanwhile, the Fife Adventurers had lost their enthusiasm for the enterprise and sold their interest to Mackenzie of Kintail. He promptly invaded Lewis and crushed all opposition, so that the island was later described as "dispeopled". In 1623 Mackenzie of Kintail became Earl of Seaforth, taking his title from this latest territory.

*   *   *

However, of all the predators who used lowland writ and influence to annexe the territories of their highland neighbours, the Campbells were the most successful – and in addition to their eastward expansion into the inland glens, in the West the old lands of the forfeited Lordship offered rich pickings as the power of the once great Clan Donald began to decline. The divisions within the Lordship and the bellicosity of the clan chiefs provided an excuse for the powerful Campbell lords, already bent on a policy of acquisitive opportunism, to intervene legally on the government's behalf – and an irresistible temptation to instigate further trouble on their own account. Thus in 1625, Sir Alexander Hay, the Clerk Register, would comment: "The frequent insurrections in the first fifteen years of the seventeenth century were encouraged if not originated by Argyll and the Campbells for their own purposes" – and Alasdair MacGregor of Glenstrae was not the only highland chief on his way to execution to make the same complaint.

In some cases, circumstances played into Argyll's hands. The MacIains of Ardnamurchan became exposed through the legal process of feudalism. A MacIain heiress had resigned the superiority of Ardnamurchan to Gillespie Grumach, Earl of Argyll, although the male heir continued to occupy the lands. In 1602, however, he was obliged to resign the estates to Argyll on the condition, as he thought, that they would be regranted to him in feu. Instead, Argyll leased Ardnamurchan to Campbell of Barbeck. The MacIains rebelled unsuccessfully, and took to piracy. Lord Lorne, Argyll's son and successor, forcibly cleared them out of Ardnamurchan in 1625.

However, the principal objective of Campbell policy in the western highlands and islands was the ruin of the Clan Iain Mhor of Yle (the MacDonalds of Islay and Dunyveg) whose hereditary lands in Islay, Jura and Kintyre had legally become Crown territory upon the forfeiture of the Lordship of the Isles – leaving the MacDonalds as "kindly tenants".

With the death of Donald Dubh in 1545, the male line of the Lords of the Isles had been extinguished. The great territories of the old Lordship became fragmented as the various vassal clans broke free of the previous federation and the separate branches of the Clan Donald itself developed independent policies of their own.

Of these, the Clan Donald South – of Islay and Dunyveg – was the most important. This clan had remained neutral during Donald Dubh's final and hopeless bid to revive the Lordship[48], but because their founder John Mhor had been married to the heiress of the Glens of Antrim, this connection had caused them to be drawn into the rebellion of the native Irish against the English government in Ireland. This Irish involvement resulted in a serious drain on their available manpower, so that it was questionable whether the clan was strong enough to populate and hold both Islay and Kintyre. Such was their situation when at the end of the 16th century they became engaged in a particularly bloody feud with MacLean of Duart, while within the Clan Donald of Islay itself a division between the chief Angus Og and his son Sir James of Dunyveg was to prove catastrophic.[49] Both circumstances gave Argyll the opportunity to intervene.

The Crown itself was arguably the real instigator of these troubles. Seeing in the MacLeans a useful counter to the power of the Clan Donald, the government had granted a lease of the Rhinns of Islay to MacLean of Duart while ordering Angus Og to remove his people from Kintyre – the which, given the strategic importance of these areas in controlling communications with Ireland, Angus Og had no mind to concede. As part of the process of persuasion, he was imprisoned and his bail set at £20,000 – a sum which he patently could not find, and the money was advanced to him (with an ominous philanthropy) by Campbell of Cawdor (son of the murdered man who had befriended the MacGregors), who thereby acquired a financial interest in Islay (and also in Gigha).

When Angus still did not evacuate Kintyre, his son Sir James, who had been held hostage against his father's compliance, was sent to persuade him since it was known that given the MacDonalds' shortage of manpower, he was in favour of ceding Kintyre in order to keep Islay. There followed a bitter quarrel between father and son, while the Campbells played each off against the other and both against the MacLeans. Sir James imprisoned his father and drove the MacLeans out of Islay in a bloody battle at the head of Loch Gruinard in which MacLean of Duart and many of his followers were killed, but Sir James was also severely wounded by an arrow. However, his plan to withdraw his clan from Kintyre in return for a charter to Islay, although approved by the Privy Council, was never put into effect. In 1606 Angus Og retaliated by seizing Sir James and turning him over to be again imprisoned in Edinburgh while he put forward alternative proposals which would have left the Clan Donald in continued possession of their "kindly rowmes" in Kintyre – which not surprisingly were thwarted by Argyll.

This prevention of any settlement had the predictable result that in 1607 Argyll obtained a feu charter of the Clan Donald's lands in Kintyre and Jura – with the stipulation that no MacDonald could thenceforth occupy them as tenants. Subsequently the whole of Kintyre (except for Knapdale) was settled as the Lordship of Kintyre upon the Earl of Argyll and feu duty temporarily discharged on condition that he founded a "burgh... to be inhabited by Lowland men".

Islay fell to the Campbells shortly thereafter. In 1612, Angus Og was so financially reduced that he was obliged to sell Islay to Campbell of Cawdor for the paltry sum of 600 merks. An incident in 1612 enabled the Campbells to take physical possession. In that year, a bastard son of Angus called Ranald Og ("a vagabond fellow without any residence") seized the weakly guarded castle of Dunyveg, but it was quickly recaptured by another Angus Og, younger son of Angus the chief and junior brother of Sir James of Dunyveg. Angus Og intended to return the fortress to the Crown when, as he later maintained at his trial, he received a message that "the Earl of Argyll was afraid that he and his friends would give up the castle and that if they did so it would be to their utter wreck". He therefore refused to submit unless he was promised a seven year lease of the Crown lands in Islay. (The pattern seems familiar.) Andrew Knox, Bishop of the Isles whom the government sent to mediate reported to the Privy Council that "Angus Og their captain, affirmed in the hearing of many witnesses that he got direction from the Earl of Argyll to keep still the house and that the Earl should procure him therefore the whole lands of Islay and the house of Dunyveg to himself." The Bishop was no friend to the MacDonalds whom he descibed as "a false generation and a bloody people", but nor did he approve of the Campbells' strategy: "neither I nor any man who knows the state of the country (Islay) think it good or profitable to his Majesty or to the realm to make the name of Campbell greater in the Isles than they are already; nor yet to root out one pestiferous clan and plant another little better."

In the meanwhile, Sir James of Dunyveg writing from prison, offered to pay 8000 merks annual rent for Islay or else transport his kinsmen to Ireland if the government would give him money to rent lands in Antrim. But Argyll had created his opportunity and Campbell of Cawdor was given an official commission to take Islay by force.

Angus Og might still have surrendered and survived, but he received another message, allegedly from the Chancellor of Scotland, the Earl of Dunfermline, advising that if he yielded Dunyveg to himself (the Chancellor) proceedings against him would be suspended. When Angus agreed to this, a second message instructed him to occupy the castle as its official Constable and to refuse any demands for its surrender until he received further orders from the Chancellor. (Dunfermline and Argyll subsequently denied any part or knowledge of such correspondence.) When Angus therefore defied Cawdor's summons the Campbells bombarded the castle into submission. Many of the defenders were summarily put to death and Angus and his closest advisers were sent to

Edinburgh for trial. In 1615, shortly before Angus was duly executed, Sir James escaped from prison and retook Islay, but Argyll with the help of government troops and some English warships quickly put down his brief rebellion. Sir James escaped to Spain and eventually died an exile in London. "Thus ended the last great struggle of the once powerful Clan Donald of Islay and Kintyre to retain from the grasp of the Campbells these ancient possessions of their tribe" concluded Donald Gregory in his "History of the Western Highlands".

In the meanwhile, the government was pursuing new policies aimed at highland "improvement". In 1609 the Privy Council had arranged for the most prominent highland chiefs to be kidnapped aboard a government frigate and forced to sign "The Band and Statutes of Iona". "The special cause of the great misery, barbarity and poverty into which for the present our barren country is subject (stated the preamble) has proceeded of the unnaturally deadly feuds which have been fostered among us in the past age." Chieftains' households were to be reduced in size and firearms were prohibited in the islands. Bards were to be put in the stocks as common thieves and likewise driven from the country. Every highland gentleman (owning more than 60 cows) was to send his eldest son to be educated in the lowlands and the Gaelic language was banned from schools. Each chief was to have one named residence and allowed to maintain only a single galley. Highlanders were to become temperate and the importation of wine was prohibited (whisky thereafter became the principal drink). But while these ordinances may have been intended to put an end to endemic disorder by undermining the highland culture, they did not address the continuing cause of unrest which was the attempted transference of hereditary lands from clan chiefs to alien feudal superiors.

By such means, the Campbells, even as they had encroached along the inland glens, acquired from the Clan Donald the coveted lands of Islay and Kintyre. In Islay the dereliction of Finlaggan, once the seat of the great Lords of the Isles, bears witness to their occupation. Most ironic perhaps, is the recollection that, as the man who in the end profited more than most from the bounties, fines and blood money amassed during the process of their proscription, Argyll was awarded Kintyre as recompense for the expenses which he claimed to have incurred in dutifully prosecuting the Clan Gregor.

CHAPTER 9

Epilogue

*Time is like a river made up of events which happen, and its current is
strong; no sooner does anything appear than it is swept away, and another
comes in its place and will be swept away too.*

After the execution of Alasdair MacGregor of Glenstrae, the Gregarach
acknowledged no single chief, and the various branches of the clan
followed their own independent leaders – the Clan Dughaill Ciar
becoming the most prominent. In co-operation, however, they remained
a formidable guerilla fighting force and as the government persecution
gradually grew less bitter, it was increasingly in the interests of neighbouring landlords to seek some accommodation with them – not least as a
means of securing the protection of their other tenants. The majority of
the surviving Gregarach changed their names for a variety of aliases and
settled where they could – although they did not altogether change their
ways and future heroes of highland folklore were readily identified as
MacGregors (Rob Roy used the name of Campbell but was never thought
of as anything other than a MacGregor). Others who would not conform
but chose to remain outlaws in the hills – wild men such as Gilderoy, the
Red Lad – perhaps because they were fugitive MacGregors, became the
stuff of romantic ballads that sustained the legend and heroic associations
of the clan.

History dealt a variable justice to the other main protagonists. Gillespie
Grumach, 7th Earl of Argyll, went to London after the death of his first
wife where he married a minor heiress, Anne Cornwallis (her mother
owned Earls Court) for whom he embraced Roman Catholicism, and for
which he was declared traitor and outlaw in 1618. He went to Western
Flanders, taking service under Philip III of Spain until in 1627 Charles I
reversed the sentence so that he was allowed to live the last ten years of his
life in somewhat reduced circumstances in London's Drury Lane –
rejected and evicted by his son Lord Lorne who, as 8th Earl and 1st
Marquis of Argyll, was to prove grimmer than he.

Black Duncan with the Cowl died in 1631, rich and respected, remembered for his learning and enlightenment, as a notable horse breeder, tree

planter and conservationist.

During the Civil. War the MacGregors took the royalist side, not through misplaced gratitude to a dynasty which had proscribed them and legalised their downfall, but because the association of Argyll with the Covenanters determined their response, not so much in the King's cause as against their Campbell enemy.

The clan therefore rose for the Marquis of Montrose, the King's Captain General in Scotland, under Alasdair's nephew, Patrick Roy of Glenstrae, and in 1645 were rewarded with Montrose's written promise that their lands would be restored:

1645, June 7th

Whereas the Laird of MacGregor and his friends have declared themselves faithfullie for his Majestie and doe follow us in his service These air therfor be power and warrand granted be his Majestie to us to certify and assure theme, that whatsoever lands and possessions belonged justlie to his friends and their predecessors and ar now in the possession of Rebells and Enemys to his Majestie's service; They and their Heirs shall have the same Disdponed to them and confirmed be his Majestie under his hand and seal, when it shall please God to put an end to these present troubles, Providing always that the said Laird of McGregor and his said friends and their forsaids continow faithfull and constant in his Majestie's service, otherwise these presents shall be null.

Subscribed at Kinady in Cromar, the seventh day of June One thousand sex hundreth fourtie fyve yeires.

MONTROSE

A week later Charles I lost the Battle of Naseby. In September Montrose was defeated at Philiphaugh and the royalist cause went down.

The restoration of Charles II, and shortly after, the execution of the Marquis of Argyll, gave the MacGregors fresh hope for the restitution of their lands and birthright. The Statute against the Gregarach was repealed: "considering that those who were formerly designed by the name MacGregor and had, during the troubles carried themselves with such loyalty and affection to his Majestie as might justly wipe off all memory of their former miscarriages."

But Charles II did not keep the pledge – being swayed in his turn by a perceived need to counter the power of Argyll by accommodating Sir John Campbell of Glenorchy (descendant of Black Duncan and later 1st Earl of

Breadalbane). Described by a contemporary as "a man of fair complexion, grave as a Spaniard, cunning as a fox, wise as a serpent but slippery as an eel", the restitution of the MacGregor homelands was no part of his agenda.

In 1685, the execution of the 2nd Marquis of Argyll for rebellion against the Crown might have offered another chance, but Archibald the 3rd Marquis returned from exile in Holland to take part in the Revolution of 1688 in support of Willam of Orange who created him Duke of Argyll in 1701. (The MacGregors by contrast had turned out for James II – the young Rob Roy was present at the Battle of Killiekrankie.) Upon Argyll's influence the punitive legislation against the MacGregors was reinstated in the Statute Book.

Not until 1774 were the penal laws against the Clan Gregor repealed by Act of Parliament, and a few years later the head of the long disinherited branch descended from Duncan Ladasach – The Children of the Mist – was recognised as chief of the whole clan. By that time Culloden had broken the fighting strength of the highland clans. The Clearances would disperse them and the old Gaelic warrior society was tamed in the end, not by proscription or the gallows, but by a contrived pageantry and regalia readily adopted by a lowland culture, which exploits the quaintness of the highlands but owes little to the ancient Gaelic civilisation of which the lowlanders were once so contemptuous and afraid.

The MacGregors as a clan refused to die, but there was much that was forfeit forever. Chiefly, they had lost the most ancient birthright of a Celtic people to their homeland, for the Glens of MacGregor are MacGregor's no more. Do not look for the Gregarach today in Dunan or Roro or Balloch. At Dalmally a new building stands on the site of the ancient Church of Dysart in Glenorchy where once twelve MacGregor chieftains lay buried in sculptured stone cists beside the high altar. In the churchyard outside, time has erased the older inscriptions and most of the gravestones commemorate the lives of Campbells – although many of the ghosts who haunt the place might answer to another name.

Glenstrae is lonely and deserted now. The old settlements have disappeared into the peat and heather. Where the River Orchy runs into Loch Awe, there is no ruin at Stronmelochan. On its promontary at the head of the loch, the towers of Kilchurn seem picturesque and innocent on a highland summer's evening.

FINIS

Footnotes

1 Campbells of Loudoun
2 Black Book of Taymouth, p.2
3 *The Lords of the Isles* (Ronald Williams)
4 *Archaeologica Scotica*, p.141
5 *Black Book of Taymouth*, p.64, 160,177ff: Chronicle of Fortingall 1545
6 *Black Book of Taymouth*, p.155,177,189-90; Chronicle of Fortingall 1552; *Red and White Book of Menzies*, p.180
7 *Black Book of Taymouth*, p.200ff; *Red and White Book of Menzies*, p.181; *Lairds of Glenlyon* (D. Campbell), p.184–5; *Archaeologica Scotica*, p.147
8 Chronicle of Fortingall 1563; *Black Book of Taymouth*, p.206–8; *Red and White Book of Menzies*, p.171, 188, 195; *Register of the Privy Council of Scotland (RPC)* vol i, p.289
9 *RPC* i, p.228f,256f; *Black Book of Taymouth*, p.209–12; Chronicle of Fortingall 1565
10 *RPC* i, p.256, 269, 361, 390; *Red and White Book of Menzies*, p.202
11 *Archaeologica Scotica*, p.147; *Black Book of Taymouth*, p.213; Breadalbane Papers; *Red and White Book of Menzies*, p.203; Chronicle of Fortingall 1570
12 *The Clans Septs and Regiments of the Scottish Highlands* (F. Adams), p.354
13 Ibid,p.355
14 Ibid,p.353
15 *Rob Roy MacGregor: His Life and Times* (W.H. Murray); for descriptions of highland life, p.1–52
16 Breadalbane Paters, Reports of the Historical Manuscripts Commission
17 *Montrose, Cavalier in Mourning* (Ronald Williams) p.161–2; *The Heather and The Gale* (Ronald Williams) p.89–91
18 *The Book of the Thanes of Cawdor*, p.186–9; *Black Book of Taymouth*, p.242–3
19 *RPC* iv, p.509,541,556
20 Breadalbane Papers i, p.179 (Hist Man Comm)
21 *Gregory in Archaeologica Scotica*, p.46
22 *Highland Papers* i p.180ff (Scottish History Society)
23 *Lords of the Isles* (Ronald Williams)
24 *History of the Earldom of Sutherland* (Sir John Gordon), Spalding Club, ii, p.93, iv, p.238–41
25 *Domestic Annals of Scotland* (Chambers – abridged) p.128
26 *Diary of Robert Birrel 1532–1605* (Dalyell's Fragments of Scottish History);

Memoirs of Affairs in Scotland 1577–1603 (David Moysie: – Maitland Club); Annals op cit p.128–9

27 *Highland Papers*, i, p.180ff

28 *History of the Western Highlands and Islands of Scotland* (Donald Gregory) p.252

29 *The Heather and the Gale* (Ronald Williams) p.12ff

30 *Scottish Criminal Trials* (Pitcairn), i, p.391-2; *Birrell's Diary*, 2 March 1596; *Black Book of Taymouth* p.251

31 *RPC* v, p.41,74,734

32 Hugh MacDonald of Sleat (Highland Papers SHS)

33 Acts Parlt Scot. iii, p.461ff

34 *RPC* v, p.213

35 *RPC* v,p.741

36 Pitcairn op cit, ii, p.434

37 *RPC* vi, p.20, 72–3, 78, 81, 89, 101, 639

38 *Alasdair's Confession*, Pitcairn op cit, ii, p.435

39 Ibid

40 *RPC* vi,p.101,184,215,416

41 *RPC* vi, p.216

42 *RPC* vi,p.402-4

43 *Alasdair's Confession*, Pitcairn op cit

44 *Earldom of Sutherland* (Sir Robert Gordon) p.246-7

45 Pitcairn op cit,p.438

46 *Argyll, Adventures in Legend* (Marquis of Lorne) p.206ff

47 Pitcairn op cit, ii, p.434

48 *The Lords of the Isles* (Ronald Williams) p.234–47

Select Bibliography

As reflected by the Footnotes, the principal sources are:

The Black Book of Taymouth edited by Cosmo Innes for the Bannatyne Club
Archaeologica Scotica vol iv – Gregory's "Historical Account of the Clan Gregor"
The Register of the Privy Council of Scotland (RPC)
The Red and White Book of Menzies
Chronicle of Fortingall
The Reports of the Historical Manuscripts Commission Breadalbane Papers
The New Statistical Account of Scotland (1841)
The Book of the Thanes of Cawdor
History of the Earldom of Sutherland Sir Robert Gordon, Spalding Club
Domestic Annals of Scotland Chambers
Scottish Criminal Trials Pitcairn
Highland Papers Vol i Scottish History Society
History of the Western Highlands and Islands of Scotland Gregory

Besides the old classic, *History of Clan Gregor* by A.G.M. MacGregor (1898), among more recent works, I have drawn on A.A.W. Ramsay's *The Arrow of Glenlyon* (1930) and Ian Grimble's *Clans and Chiefs* (1980) while for descriptions of life in the highlands I have relied heavily on W.H. Murray's excellent book *Rob Roy MacGregor – His Life and Times* (1982).

Index

Index

MacKay of Strathnaver, Clan, 79–82
  Aodh, 81
  Donald of Farr, 81
  Uisdean, 81
Mackenzie, Clan, 84–5
Mackenzie of Kintail, 84–5 (*see also*
  Earls of Seaforth)
MacKinnon, Clan, 4
MacLean of Duart, Clan, 9, 36, 61, 87
  Lachlan, 41, 47, 55
MacLeod of Dunvegan and Lewis,
  Clan, 84–5
MacNab, Clan, 4
MacPherson, Clan, 40, 47
MacQuarrie, Clan, 4
Maitland, John, Lord Thirlestane,
  Chancellor, 37, 41, 44, 52
Mary, Queen of Scots, 20, 21, 22, 80
Menzies of Weem, 11, 15, 16, 53, 74
  Sir Robert of that Ilk, 16, 20, 21,
  41
Montrose, James Graham, Marquis
  of, 91
Moray, Earls of, 40, 80
  Archibald Douglas, 39
  George, 4th Earl of Huntly, 39
  James Stewart (Regent), 39
  James, "The Bonnie Earl", 40–4,
  45, 47
  John Dunbar, 39
  Thomas Randolph, 39
Murray of Atholl, Clan, 4, 9

Murray of Tullibardine, John, 55–7,
  59

Rannoch, (District), 4, 15, 16, 17, 21,
  37, 55, 62, 65, 76
Robert I, The Bruce, 2, 7, 13, 61, 79
Roberston (Clan Donnachaidh), 16,
  17
Rossdhu, 61, 62, 63, 64

Schiehallion, 12, 22, 76
Semple of Fulwood, 63
Sinclair, *see* Caithness Earls of;
Stewart, Francis, Earl of Bothwell, 42
Stewart, James, Regent, Earl of
  Moray, 39, 80
Stewart of Appin, 41, 47
Stewart of Ardvorlich, 32–3, 49, 69
Stewart of Garth, 9, 12
Stewart of Lorne, 3
Strathnaver, 79–80
Stronfernan, 15, 37
Stronmilchan (Stronmelochan), 13,
  60, 92
Sutherland, Earls of, 79–82
  Alexander Gordon, 81–2
  John Gordon, 80–1

Trossachs, 4, 15

Wallace, Sir William, 2, 13

99

Also by Ronald Williams

The Heather and the Gale

Clan Donald and Clan Campbell during the Wars of Montrose

After the forfeiture of the Lordship of the Isles two mighty families Clan Donald and Clan Campbell emerged as prominent amongst those who sought to fill the power vacuum in the West of Scotland. Ronald Williams shows how their differing strategies led inexorably to that fatal confrontation, wherein Gaeldom, Catholicism and the King were eventually overwhelmed by Calvinism and bloody revolution. He sweeps through the saga of Montrose's campaign with a vigour and passion that is as infectious as it is stimulating.

220 pages including 9 maps.
ISBN 1 899863 18 4
£11.99

Available from:
House of Lochar
Isle of Colonsay
Argyll PA61 7YR
Scotland

http://www.colonsay.org.uk/lochar.html